Brutal Jogle

NO EASY DAY

JOHN O' GROATS TO LAND'S END SELF-SUPPORTED

CLAIRE SMITH

Dedicated to Susan Northcott
An amazing woman we all loved so very much

Foreword

I was out running during lockdown and thinking about my best friend's mum, Susan Northcott, who had recently passed away with cancer. Susan had been a very positive role model for me when I was growing up. She was strong, feisty, and always looking for adventures. She was never one to shy away from tough situations or say what she thought. Her death had been sudden, and I missed her. I hadn't been able to go to her funeral due to COVID-19 restrictions, which was hard. I felt like I hadn't been able to say goodbye properly.

Whilst I ran, I remembered a book Susan had bought me called 'The Clock Keeps Ticking' by Sharon Gayter. The book details Sharon's record-breaking run (recently broken by Carla Moninaro) from John o' Groats to Land's End in 12 days and 11 hours. Although I could never aspire to running from John o' Groats to Land's End (also known as 'JOGLE') in anywhere near that time, I wondered about taking on the distance, whether I could complete it, and how long it would take me.

I decided that running the length of the UK in Susan's memory was a fitting way to celebrate her life, and that she would have absolutely loved the idea and encouraged me all the way. I told my best friend Claire (Susan's daughter), who thought the idea was brilliant (a bit mental, but most of my ideas are) and the planning commenced.

Unfortunately, COVID-19 had brought my ultra-events business to an abrupt halt. There would be no races in 2020, which meant no revenue. Facing an uncertain future regarding my finances I would be operating on a very limited budget. But if I were to have any chance of completing the Brutal JOGLE, I still needed to make sure I had all the essentials covered: kit, hydration, food, and my own physical health.

I'm not very good at asking for things, so I initially thought that getting some sponsors on board was going to be hard. But once I got started, I was surprised at how many companies wanted to help. The first company I approached was Wiggle's DHB. They were looking for strong, female athletes to promote their brand and their 'Don't Hold Back' message. My previous ultra-distance achievements and the upcoming JOGLE challenge was definitely on point for them, so after discussing what I would need, I received a large package containing tops, leggings, socks, coats and of course, the famous DHB Visor that I became very attached to.

The second business to get involved was Resilient Nuts. This was particularly exciting for me, because I was concerned about how I would find enough calories when covering the 900 or so miles of the JOGLE. Their long-range fuel is super energy dense; as it's mainly nut butter, there are no sugar-spiking issues, and the natural protein would help with muscle repair. The company was only just starting up, so as with DHB, they were looking for a wide range of ultra-distance ambassadors. Their sponsored athletes included the amazing Vendée Globe sailor Pip Hare, and Tom Warburton who was training to walk solo to the South Pole. To help promote their brand, 'The Nutter Team' sent me all the sachets I would need and some other freebies too. Their nutritional expert, Greg Potter, also helped me devise a plan to get through the challenge.

Precision Hydration were the third company to support me. I have known the founder, Andy Blow, for about 10 years and I have always respected him. He is not only a sports scientist, but also an accomplished athlete as well. He set up Precision Hydration to tailor electrolyte tablets to suit athlete's needs. To do this, he developed a sweat testing device to establish how much athletes sweat and therefore what level of electrolyte replacement they would require. As I suspected, I barely sweat at all (I'm permanently cold) and would normally use the lowest level of tablet, PH 500. But for the Brutal JOGLE, Andy advised I took one PH 1500 tablet per day, due to the fact I would be pushing myself for such a long period.

Andy Blow also kindly put me in touch with the final company to sponsor me, Melio Health. I was very keen to get some before and after blood tests to show what (if anything) these types of arduous events do to the body from a physiological perspective. I had a Zoom call with Andy the Managing Director, and Kush and Joel (two of the doctors), before the challenge. Andy then arranged for me to go to Harley Street for the blood tests. Driving up to London before the event was exciting, although a little stressful trying to find parking near the private clinic. Driving up a few days after the event was not so fun! Especially as I had to be fasted for the bloods tests and I was permanently starving for the following weeks after I had finished.

I had another Zoom call with the team after we had the results back, and Kush and Joel were extremely helpful with advising me on going forward with certain aspects of improving my overall health.

My team

Kathi Harman is my event photographer and very good friend. She took on the role of social media co-ordinator and general go-to person for people to contact if they had a question or wanted to meet me along the route. She also helped with promoting the charity that I had chosen to raise money for, the Forest Holme hospice where Susan stayed at the end of her life. Kathi did an excellent job, and she was also one of the people who held up my morale when things got tough. Which was frequently.

Gavin Jeffers has been taking part in The Brutal Extreme Triathlons for a long time, finally building to the Double Iron distance a few years ago. We had become friends and I loved his dry sense of humour and funny Facebook posts. He had chatted to me before my challenge about going over the Pentlands, which was his local training ground. This was an area of hills near Edinburgh that I would have to cross. Gavin had messaged me with his concerns about the buggy and the suitability of the route I had chosen. He sent me an alternate course and by doing that became involved in the Brutal JOGLE. I'm not sure it was his intention, but sometimes these things just happen…

Kathi and Gavin became my Brutal Basecamp. Within the Facebook messenger group, they supported, cajoled, made fun of, sent love and inappropriate jokes and basically were the people I talked to the most during the challenge. They knew when to take the piss out of my whining and tell me to man up. But they also sensed when something was serious and I needed people to vent or cry to.

Another person who has been a rock of support to me over the years was my friend Matthew Dales. Matthew won the first ever Double Brutal in 2012, then came out of ultra-distance retirement to finish 3rd in the Continuous UK Deca, 2019. He has spent the best part of a decade hiking, climbing and cycling around the globe, giving him a wealth of experience in self-supported travel. During my JOGLE attempt I would often phone Matthew during the evening whilst I was walking along a quiet lane or through a small village, and depending on what state I was in, he would offer words of encouragement or tell me stories of his adventures to take my mind off the endless miles that lay ahead and the pain in my feet. I loved our phone calls.

My family and friends were a huge support as well. My mum was glued to the tracker and always messaged me when I went into a shop (what are you buying?) or when I stopped for the night in some random field (are you sleeping?). Also, my good friend and business partner James Page, who surprised me with a visit one day as I was running along a bike path and who phoned me regularly during the challenge to check on my progress and mental state. James has completed the Double and Triple Brutal Triathlons, is a Deca Ironman finisher, and has also cycled LEJOG-JOGLE (Land's End to John o' Groats, then back to Land's End) with his son.

I was simply blown away by the amount of support I received via social media and when friends, Brutal competitors, and also complete strangers, would find me and say hello along the route. For someone who is a little introverted, I actually really loved meeting everyone, and the energy that they would leave was tangible and became invaluable to me.

As much as this was a self-supported* JOGLE attempt, the cheers, beeps, COVID-19 unsafe hugs, messages and comments that I received from people over 24 days was wonderfully life affirming and kept me ticking the miles off, day after day, despite the constant challenges I faced.

Note on self-supported definition: *Self-Supported means you may have as much support as you can manage or find along the way, but not from any pre-arranged people helping you. This can range from caching supplies in advance, purchasing supplies along the way, to finding or begging for food or water.* I accepted food/drink offered to me by strangers along the route, talked to anyone I met who was interested in what I was doing, phoned friends/family along the way if I needed help, advice, or just a chat, and occasionally slept in hotels as well as my trusty tent. I used bike shops for jogger spares and repairs.

The Brutal Buggy

When I first came up with the idea to attempt the JOGLE, it had been my plan to run with a rucksack. Having completed a Double Fan Dance (mountain race in Wales, made famous for its use in Special Forces selection) the previous year with a 25lb pack, I knew this would be very challenging but thought it doable. I decided to complete a fully loaded test run along the South West Coast Path before my JOGLE attempt, from Lyme Regis back to my hometown of Christchurch. This was around 100 miles and, in hindsight, much too far to run so close to my JOGLE start date.

Despite only making it to mile 50 (the injuries were accumulating and started to put the whole challenge at risk), the training weekend was a success. The main thing I learnt was that attempting the JOGLE with a pack would be a very bad idea. Running with 35lbs on my small frame was ridiculously slow and painful, to the extent that I risked permanently damaging my back. I also learnt that I would require something more substantial than a bivy bag to sleep in. The length of time that I would be on the road meant that I needed enough space each night to sort my kit and fix my feet, not to mention cooking and recovery. I simply could not do this in a bivy bag, so needed to find an alternative. Fortunately I had recently met a fellow adventurer, Darren Hardy, who kindly offered to lend me his awesome RAB Latok tent for the challenge. The tent was not much heavier than my bivy, and it meant that I could have the space I needed at the end of each day.

But how was I going to carry my kit? Weight would be a big factor on the challenge, so I knew I had to lighten my load as much as possible. I went through everything I needed, over and over again, but I could not see a way to reduce it. I knew I needed a decent warm jacket and waterproofs because I felt the cold so much; there was no way I could leave those behind. I also needed a gas stove, fuel, and dehydrated meals. I would carry some basic snacks to ensure I always had emergency calories with me. Alongside those were medical supplies, spare trainers, a few extra items of warm clothing and fresh socks. Battery packs were a must, too. I didn't want my GPS devices or phone to run out of power in the middle of nowhere. Then there was a pair of flip-flops, charging cables, tools, two head torches, bug spray and a mosquito net. And finally, I had to pack my sleeping bag, camping mat and tent.

It was a lot of kit and carrying it on my back for so long was clearly not an option. I began to look at pulks (land versions of the type of sled pulled by Arctic explorers) and after a bit of research stumbled across a company called Aiguille Alpine Equipment in the Lake District. The owner of the shop, Adrian, was very helpful and told me that I didn't need a pulk, but a trailer instead. He went on to say that he had one I could borrow, but I would need to collect it. The following week I made the long drive up to Cumbria and returned with a worryingly heavy frame. After borrowing some mountain bike wheels, I fitted them and then attached the trailer to the harness that I had bought from Adrian. I then attached the harness around my waist and headed out into the streets for a test run.

Walking wasn't too bad. However, when I tried to run, the trailer rocked violently up and down, almost lifting me off the ground. The turning circle was also completely impractical. I knew straight away this trailer would have been fine for carrying large amounts of kit over relatively short distances, but it definitely wasn't suitable for the JOGLE.

By this point I had about a week until I left for Scotland and I was running out of options. It was time for plan C. I had already been looking at a baby jogger for sale about 10 miles from me. It was £100, and as I had owned one when my son was little, I knew it could potentially do the job. The pulk shop owner had also emailed to ask if I had considered using one, as he'd seen some ultra-runners in America using them. It was the most sensible option, but if I'm really honest I did not want to run with a push chair. Yes, it was the most practical and fastest way for me to carry my kit from one end of the country to the other, but I really didn't like the image of me, running with a baby-less buggy. However, with only seven days to go, I was out of options. I swallowed my pride and emailed the lady to say I would buy it.

Once I was the proud owner of a baby jogger for the second time in my life, I set about trying to fit everything on to the frame and small seat. It was surprisingly easy, and I managed to fit the main dry bag with all my kit in where the child would normally sit. Two square water bottles (so they wouldn't roll) were secured to the footrest with some netting from Halfords. Underneath the buggy was a perfect place for the dry bag containing my sleeping bag, tent and roll mat. All the bags were secured with bungy cords I found in my van, and I also covered the main bag with a fluorescent yellow cover for maximum visibility. I thought I'd better take it for a test run, so I ran up the road and back, making sure I bumped up and down a few curbs to see how it dealt with them. After this extremely scientific, thorough and extensive expedition road test, I concluded it would be fine. All I had to do now was order a flag from Amazon to complete the bizarre, ultra-running-crazy-lady-with-a-pushchair look I had created.

And so, six days later, I found myself standing at the famous John o' Groats signpost at 4:45am, on my own, in the dark. I was fiddling nervously with my satellite tracker, trying to work out why my location was shown as off the coast of Ghana and not Scotland*. I desperately phoned the tracker guy, hoping he would wake up and take my call to resolve the issue. He did, and five minutes later my little GPS marker pinged up with the correct location and I breathed a sigh of relief. After a few selfies and a short video for the BBC, I started my Garmin and began the longest run of my life.

*Null Island is a name for the point on the Earth's surface where the prime meridian and the equator cross, off the west African coast. This is at zero degrees latitude and longitude (0°N, 0°E).

It was my initial plan to run 52 miles a day and break the men's self-supported record of 17 days and 23 hours (there was no women's record at the time of my attempt). I knew this would always be a stretch for me as I am a plodder at the best of times, but I am always overly optimistic about my abilities. A few friends had expressed their concern over my plans, but I just shrugged and said, "what will be, will be". I had run two marathons a day during a continuous Deca in Switzerland in 2017, but that was with support and over a very simple, flat lap.

On the first day of my JOGLE attempt I managed to get within a mile of my planned 52-mile target, but it was the one and only time I did. After that, I aimed for 40 miles a day and was always pleased when I managed to reach that goal. The risk of injury was constantly on my mind, so often my pace was dictated by how my legs and feet were behaving that day. I was always careful not to push too much for fear of having to stop halfway and catch a train home (a thought that horrified me). I knew that running self-supported would be considerably harder than with a crew, but I didn't really allow for the time spent finding somewhere to camp and pitching/packing the tent. Loading and unloading the buggy also took a good 20 minutes per day. Looking after my feet and trying to dry my soggy trainers and other kit was tricky, as well as buying food and storing it so I could grab what I needed on the move. Answering messages also took time; although I didn't do too much of this, I couldn't (and didn't want to) ignore family and friends.

In short, my days involved far more than just running (and walking), and the challenge took much longer than I wanted it to. It was so much harder than I had anticipated. However, I wouldn't have changed a thing.

The Brutal JOGLE Timeline

Fri Aug 14th: Left Christchurch, Dorset with a hire car to drive to Scotland. Stayed at Hotel near Glasgow.

Sat Aug 15th: Left hotel early to drive to Inverness. Dropped off hire car and got the train to Thurso. Got a lift from future Brutal competitor to John o' Groats B&B.

Sun Aug 16th: John o' Groats to Helmsdale - **51.43 miles**
Mon Aug 17th: Helmsdale to Scotsburn - **42.74 miles**
Tues Aug 18th: Scotsburn to Auchnahillin - **37.15 miles**
Wed Aug 19th: Auchnahillin to Insh - **37.71 miles**
Thurs Aug 20th: Insh to Calvine - **37.71 miles**
Fri Aug 21st: Calvine to Moneydie - **37 miles**
Sat Aug 22nd: Moneydie to Queensferry (Forth Bridge) - **41.11 miles**
Sun Aug 23rd: Queensferry to West Linton - **23.36 miles**
Mon Aug 24th: West Linton to Beattock - **38.61 miles**
Tues Aug 25th: Beattock to Gretna (Storm Francis) - **27.95 miles**
Wed Aug 26th: Gretna to Little Strickland - **39.09 miles**
Thurs Aug 27th: Little Strickland to Natland - **23 miles**
Fri Aug 28th: Natland to Preston - **43.32 miles**
Sat Aug 29th: Preston to Stretton - **34.63 miles**
Sun Aug 30th: Stretton to Alderton - **41.67 miles**
Mon Aug 31st: Alderton to Ludlow - **39.9 miles**
Tues Sept 1st: Ludlow to Hereford - **26.71 miles**
Wed Sept 2nd: Hereford to Aust (Severn Bridge) - **40.83 miles**
Thurs Sept 3rd: Aust (Severn Bridge) to Rooks Bridge - **39.5 miles**
Fri Sept 4th: Rooks Bridge to Great Fossend - **40.5 miles**
Sat Sept 5th: Great Fossend to Okehampton - **44.7 miles**
Sun Sept 6th: Okehampton to Bodmin - **38.28 miles**
Mon Sept 7th: Bodmin to Camborne - **41.4 miles**
Tues Sept 8th: Camborne to Land's End - **24.62 miles**

Locations are to the closest town or village for reference.

Day 1: Sunday 16th August
John o' Groats to Helmsdale - 51.43 miles

I woke before my alarm went off and lay in bed for a moment. The enormity of what I was about to attempt washed over me.

I am about to try and run the length of the UK. Self-supported.

Why did I think this was a good idea? I'm not even that good at running…

I swung my legs out of bed and put the kettle on. I had an hour to sort myself out and load my kit on to the baby jogger that I was using to carry everything over the 870-ish miles of the route. As I brushed my teeth, I looked at myself in the mirror and really questioned my sanity. Where did this come from? It's not like it had been a lifelong dream to complete the JOGLE - in fact, I'd only decided to do it at the beginning of June.

Regardless of the size of the challenge and my dubious mental state, I was now just minutes away from starting. I did my final kit check, pushed the jogger outside into the chilly morning air and walked the half mile from my B&B to the legendary John o' Groats signpost and the beginning of my adventure.

I had been advised to walk the first mile as it was uphill, and after the last 24 hours of packing, driving and general stress, I suddenly felt overwhelmingly tired. Not the best way to feel the first hour in, but on that early Sunday morning there was no pressure. No crew, no messages or people watching (yet), it was just me and the buggy walking along the road. I didn't even see a car for the first hour, it was bliss.

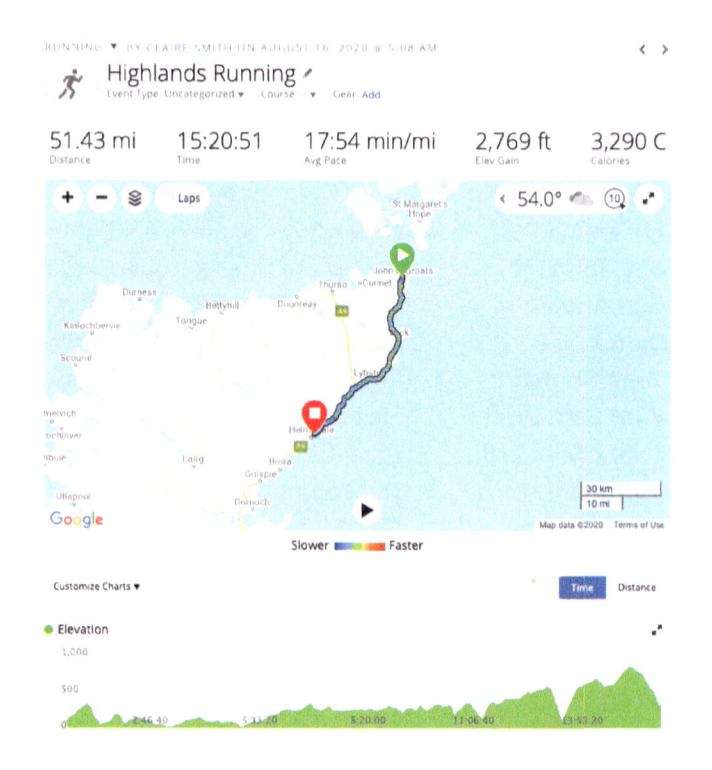

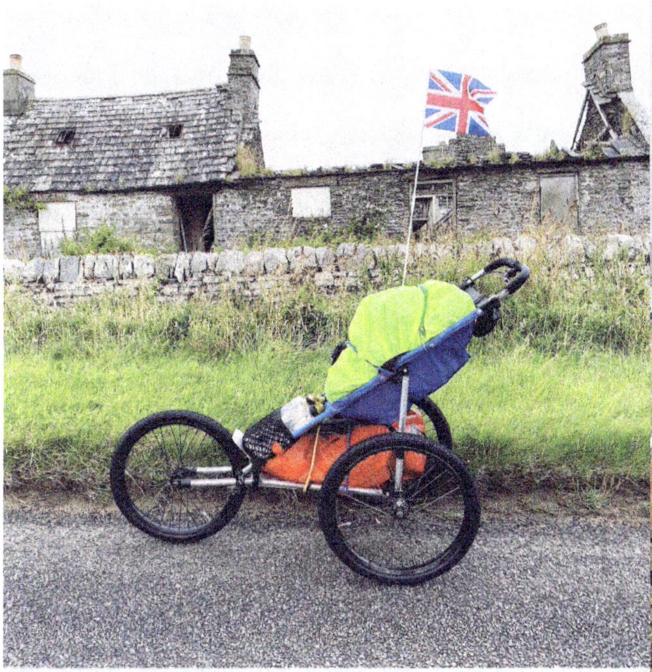

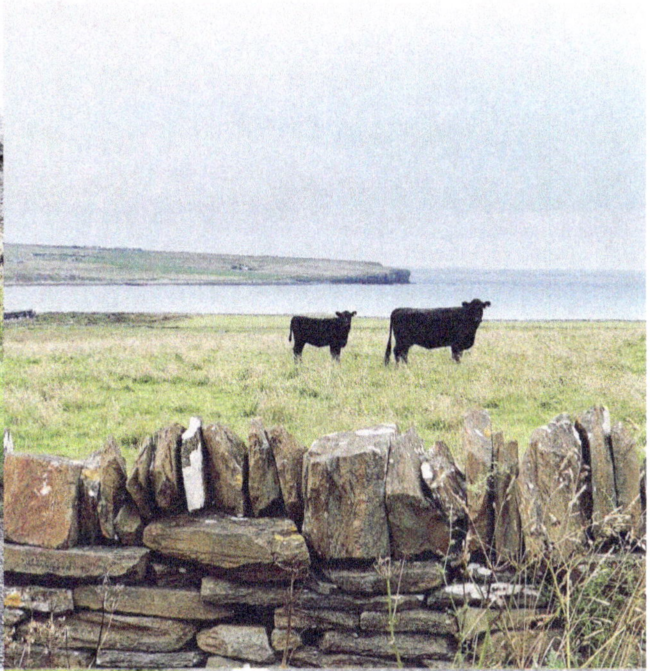

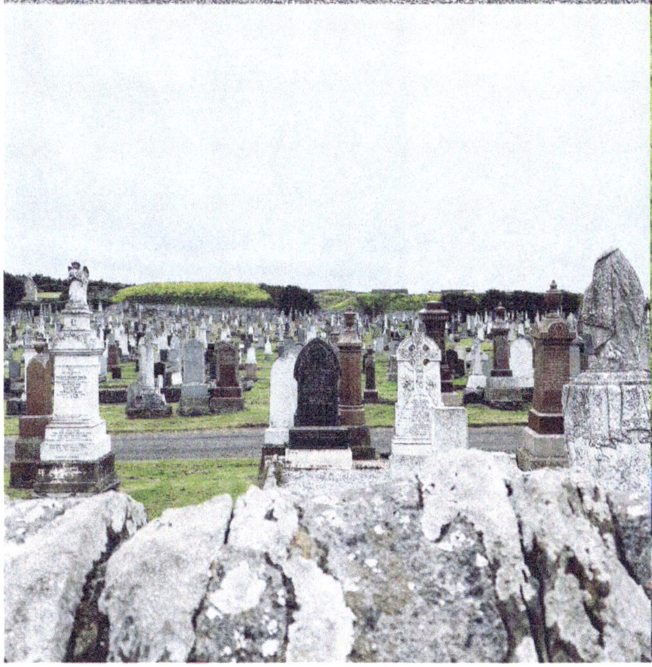

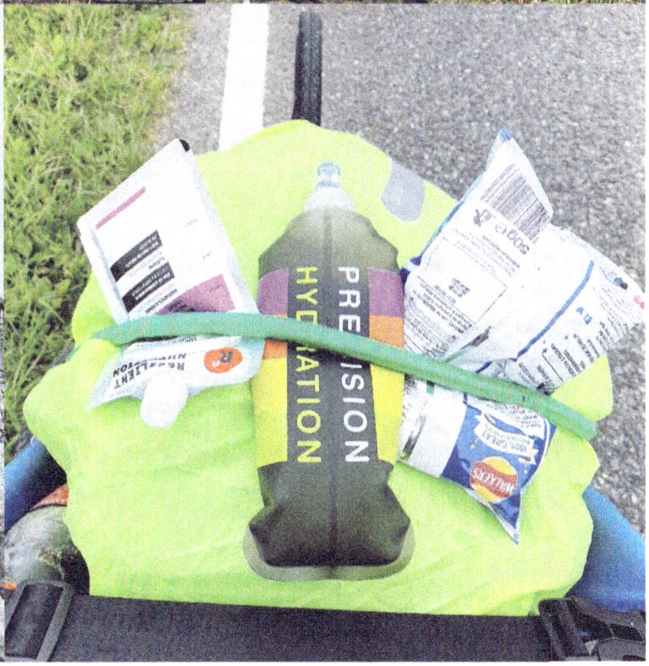
PRECISION
HYDRATION

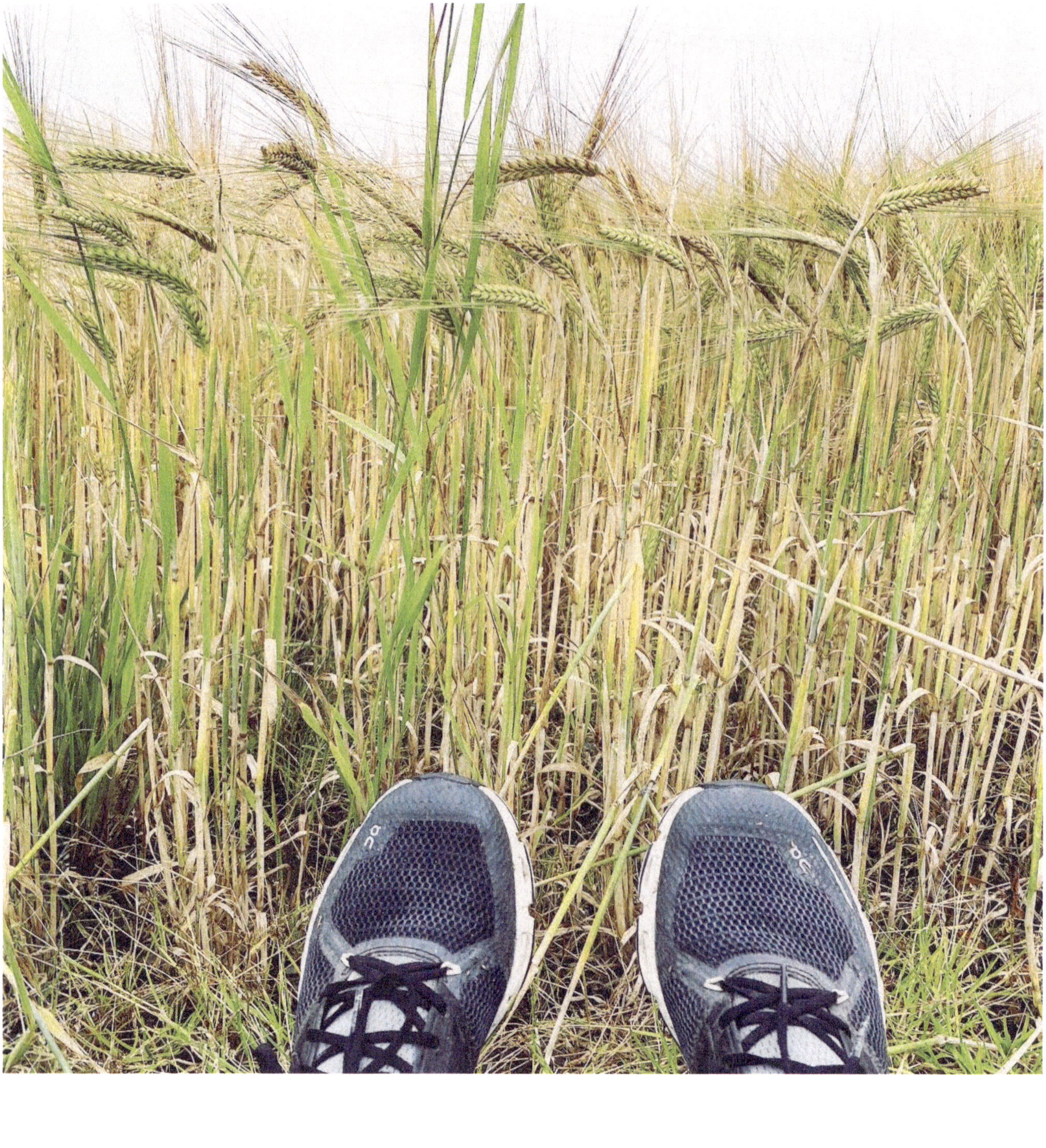

After the pressure of the build up with sponsors and social media, I felt myself start to relax as I began to run slowly, warming up my stiff muscles.

Bloody hell, I was actually in Scotland. I was actually going to run the length of the UK. I shook my head in disbelief. I've taken on some crazy challenges before, but this was one of the maddest ideas I'd had in my life.

The first part of Day 1 was spent making my way along the quiet road to Wick, where I was able to grab some lunch and refill my water bottles. I also saw my first sign for Inverness, 103 miles away. Wick gave me my first experience of people's reaction to the baby jogger and my Hi-Viz jacket, which stated that I was attempting a JOGLE world record. I had been advised by Carla Moninaro (who, very kindly, supplied me with her GPX files for the route) to wear a printed Hi-Viz to help people understand what I was doing, and in turn be more considerate. It definitely helped - God only knows how bad it would have been on the roads without it. What I quickly learnt was that most drivers didn't give a damn about my record attempt or fund raising, all they knew was that I was in their way and preventing them from getting to the next queue of traffic 10 seconds sooner. In fact, the behaviour of a huge number of drivers made what I was doing incredibly hard and shocked me on an almost hourly basis some days.

On the flip side of the impatient drivers, there were people who would literally stop and give me money, toot their horns and cheer me on. Complete strangers would ask me what I was doing and then pull out their wallet or purse and hand me notes for the charity. I had printed some cards before I left with all the website details and charity info, so I could give people something to read and share. These worked brilliantly, although they got a bit soggy with all the rain.

After Wick, the route got busier still. Then the hills started. As I had gone into this challenge somewhat under-prepared, I hadn't really spent much time training with the baby jogger. The only real running I had done with it was down the road in my flip-flops a few days before I left. I had expected it to be hard to push up hill, but I wasn't expecting to be pulled down them. The jogger did have a front brake but if the wheel bounced, I would suddenly have no brakes at all and the jogger would lurch violently away, taking me with it. If the hill was super-steep, the tyre would simply skid on the road, once again leaving me to control 40lbs of kit plus jogger which was desperately trying to escape from me.

On the first day I also experienced the huge lorries that would speed past me on the A9, leaving me blinking and breathless. I had made a Will before I'd left home, and at the time I'd thought I might be being a little over-dramatic. But as each massive 18-wheeler thundered past me, only inches away, it felt more and more like a sensible idea.

This night would be my first ever experience of wild camping and I was quite excited about it. Just before the 52-mile target, I saw a pathway that lead off the A9. I pushed the buggy off the road and saw that it led to a small, secluded area that was perfect for me and my tent. Stopping my Garmin, I unpacked the tent and set up camp. I locked the buggy up, God knows why, there was nobody around other than the relentless lorries and occasional car on the road next to where I slept.

That night was the only real time I had issues with the infamous Scottish Midges. They stopped me from cooking, as I didn't want to use my Jetboil stove in the tent (I soon got over that as the days went on) and cooking outside was impossible without getting eaten alive. Instead, I ate some cheese in my sleeping bag, quietly concerned over the number of niggles I could already feel, but also happy with what was a pretty decent start.

Day 2: Monday 17th August
Helmsdale to Scotsburn - 42.74 miles - Total mileage: 94.17

Day 2 was a massive wake up call. I had huge muscle aches from the Scottish hills. Not just from going up them, it was the downhills that had smashed my legs. I just hadn't preprepared for how hard it would be with a heavily weighted pushchair pulling me down the steep descents. Maybe I should have actually trained for this? I also had large blisters forming on the balls of my feet. This was a painful shock so early on in the challenge, as in recent long-distance events where the run sections had been on road, I rarely got any blisters. I drained and cleaned them, then applied some Compeed. This would become a daily routine.

The realisation also hit me of what I was trying to do. Run the entire length of the UK. It seemed totally doable at home. It was exciting making the plans of how many miles I could do, what I would eat, and where I would sleep. It now felt overwhelming and impossible.

What had I done? I realised that 52 miles a day, on top of everything else I had to deal with, was just not realistic. The comments of my closest friends in the weeks leading up to the JOGLE rang in my head. "Just do what you can each day" and "It's an adventure, don't put pressure on yourself". I felt a little foolish, but I always set myself crazy, high goals and never really thought about the practicalities of actually achieving them.

But that day, I had to quietly admit to myself that covering 52 miles every day for the next two weeks was not going to happen.

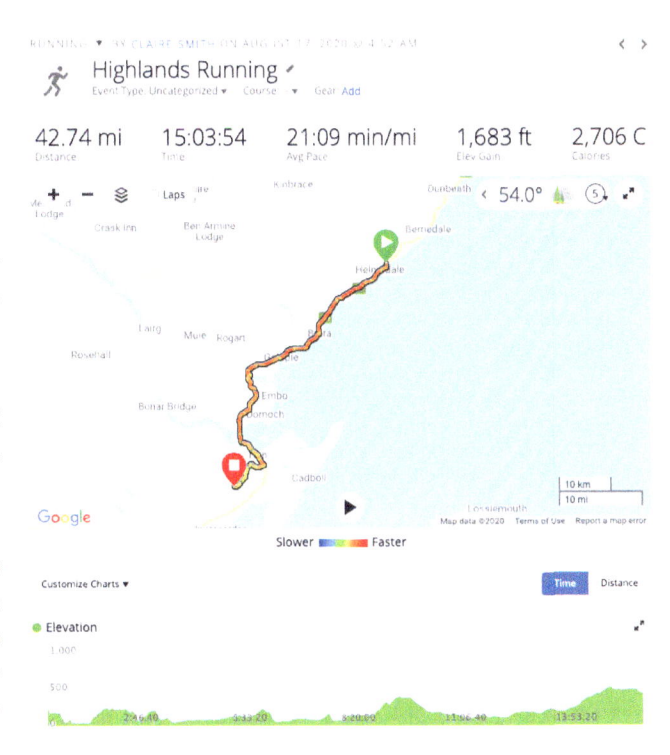

I was also struggling to eat as much as I needed to. This was a common problem with me. I'm not a huge eater in my day-to-day life and when I do these long endurance events, I tend to just eat the same amount as I normally do, with a few extra snacks thrown in. This obviously leads to low energy levels and weight loss, and I needed to try and force myself to get more calories down if I was to make it to Cornwall.

The amount of traffic increased on the A9 and I was shocked at how close people got to me, whizzing past my elbow at high speed. I eventually got on to some quieter roads and finally a lane with practically no cars at all. It was bliss, and the views around me were gorgeous. I reminded myself that what I was doing was a privilege and also my choice. My mood lifted again and I felt positive about being able to do this.

Later that day, I trotted past an older man and his daughter as they were parking up with their dog. "Hold on" he called after me, and I waited for them to catch up. Walking along with them, I explained what I was doing and gave them a card so they could follow my tracker. The man chatted to me about the local area and pointed out oil rigs in the Nigg Bay that look like something from a sci-fi movie in the mist.

After a time, they said goodbye and I was left alone again. A little while later I found a path leading off the road, with a small grassy area and picnic bench. It seemed to be the start of a public footpath and felt like a good place to camp. There were some houses close by, but I was sheltered by the hedges and it felt safe. I pitched my tent and once everything I needed was inside, I pulled out my JetBoil and one of my de-hydrated Firepot meals. By the time I had sorted my kit and feet and wriggled into my sleeping bag, the meal was ready. I started to eat, and it tasted so good. I made a mental note that I must eat more. A hot meal every night is important for recovery, but also morale.

I curled up on my sleeping mat and felt a little more prepared to take on Day 3…

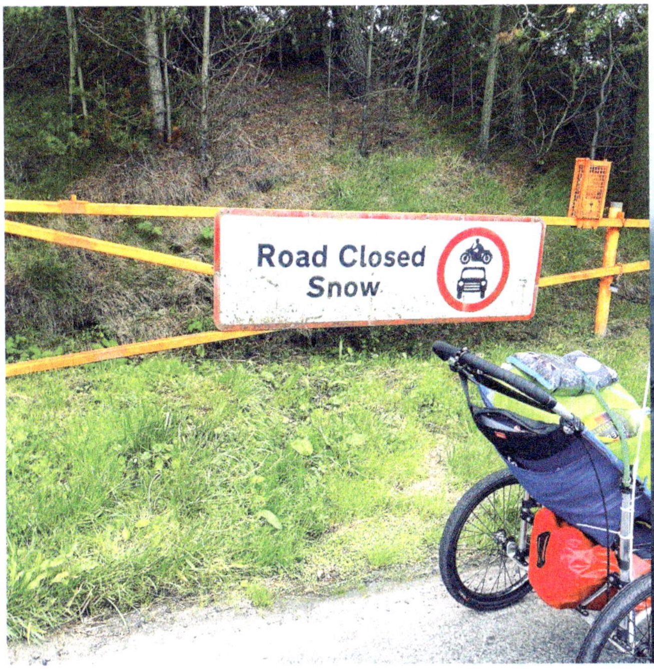
Road Closed
Snow

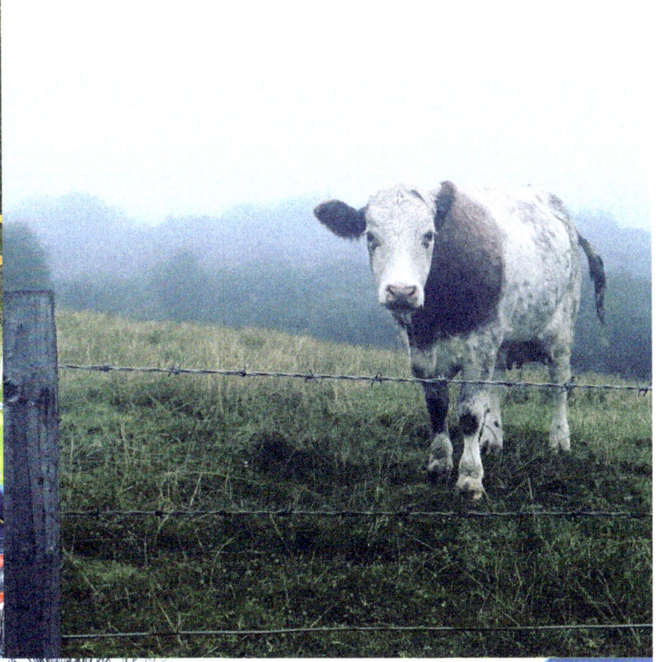

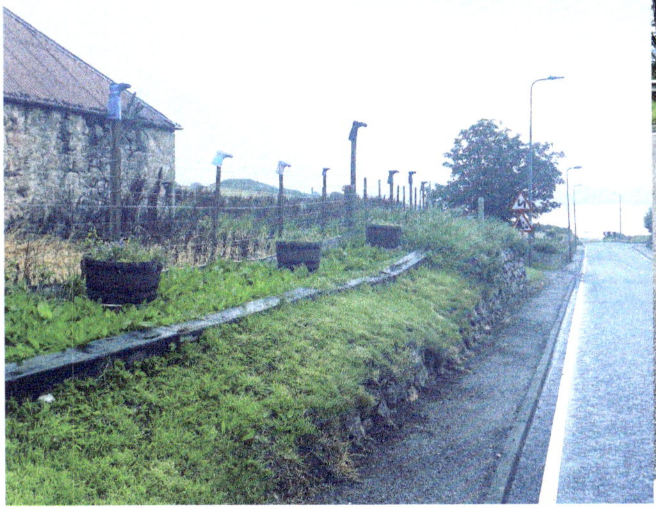

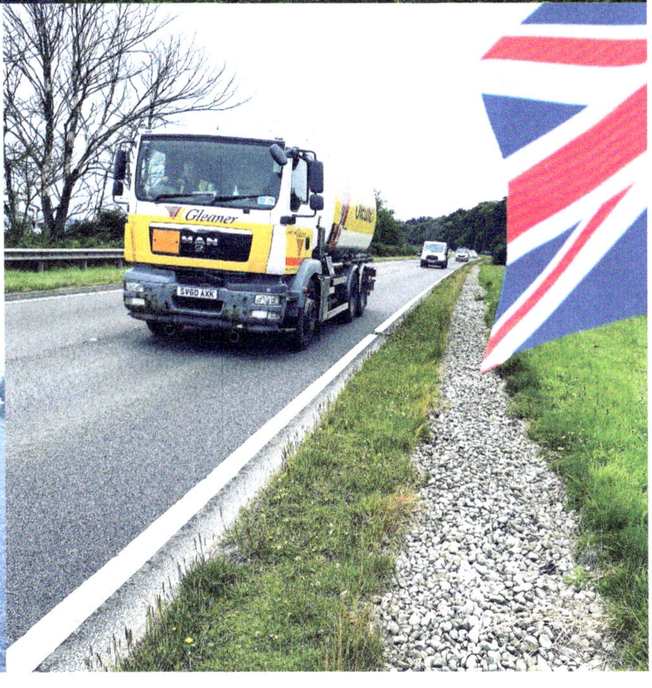
Gleaner
SV60 AXK

Day 3: 18th Tuesday August
Scotsburn to Auchnahillin - 37.15 miles - Total mileage: 131.32

Day 3 started well, on the nice country lane where I stopped the night before. The lane lead on to a slightly busier road which was still manageable, but as I got onto the A9 the carnage began. On some of the busier A roads I had still felt relatively safe, as a white line delineated a hard shoulder where I could to stay out of the main lane. Not quite a bike path, but enough for me to run along without the traffic having to stop behind or in front of me (depending on which side I was on at the time). But today, the line was right up against the verge leaving no shoulder, and the traffic was fast and unrelenting. The worst vehicles were the timber lorries carrying huge loads of lumber. They would power past me and almost knock me off my feet. They seemed to barely registered (or care) that I was on the road.

As I sat in a gateway to a field, eating a pork pie, I decided my only option to make any safe progress was to get on the verge. This was soul-destroying as there were large, rutted areas, rocks and holes hidden under the thick wet, grass. The buggy kept hitting them, making it almost impossible to get any momentum going. The road was also sloping uphill and seemed to go on for hours. In fact it was only about a mile and a half - but when you are practically parallel to the road, arms outstretched, pushing a heavy load on that surface, it felt like forever. Trying to make progress on that hill really tested me, both physically and mentally.

Once I reached the top, I crossed a bridge and the white line moved again to form another hard shoulder, allowing me to run in the road. I could have cried. Maybe I did. The volume and speed of the traffic hadn't changed, but at least I could make some real progress again.

I had been chasing the Inverness road signs since I had seen the first one back in Wick, and finally I arrived. This lifted my spirits as I felt like I was really getting somewhere. As I crossed the firth, the views were stunning. A wide expanse of water with an industrial

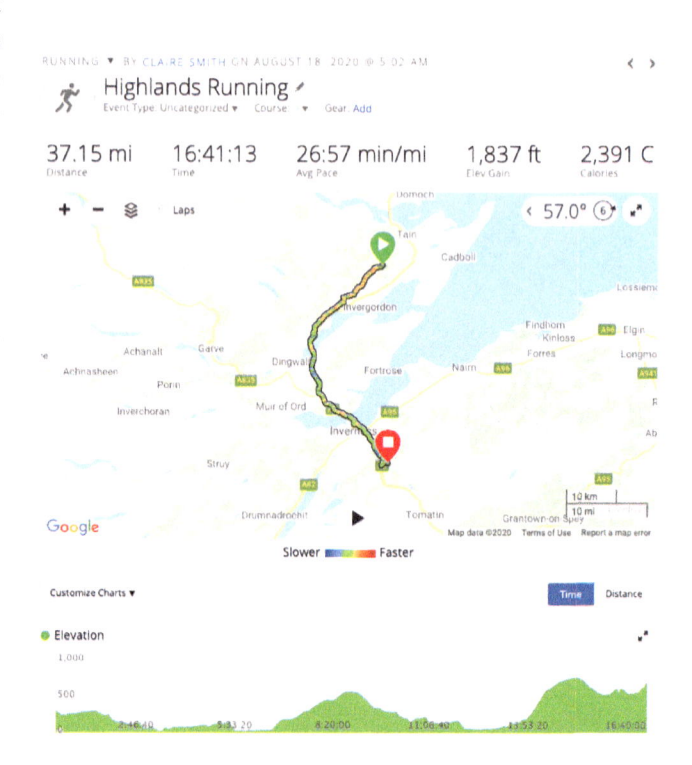

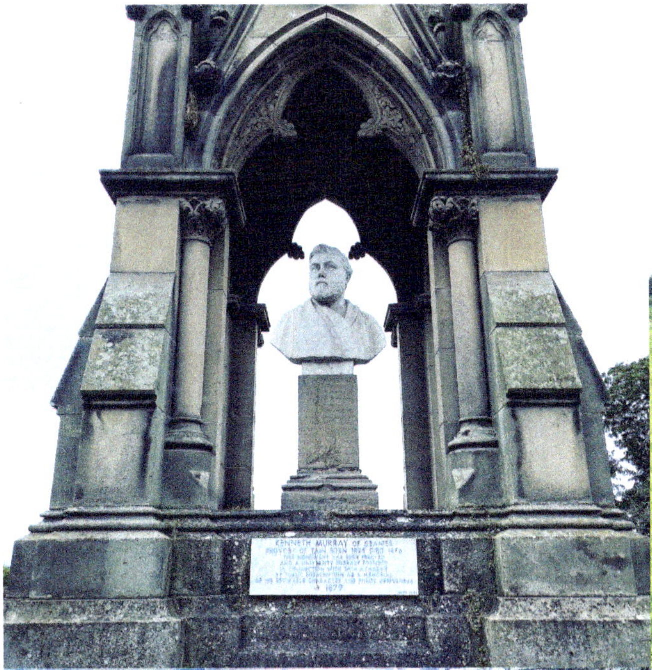
KENNETH MURRAY OF GEANIES

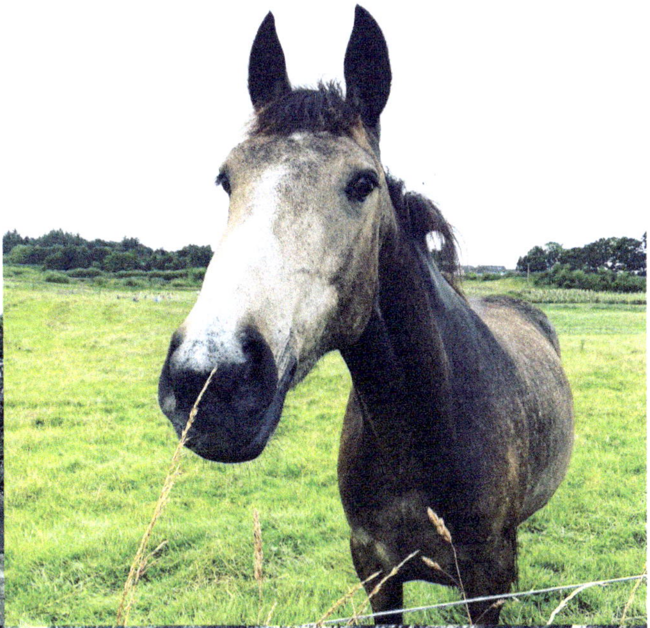

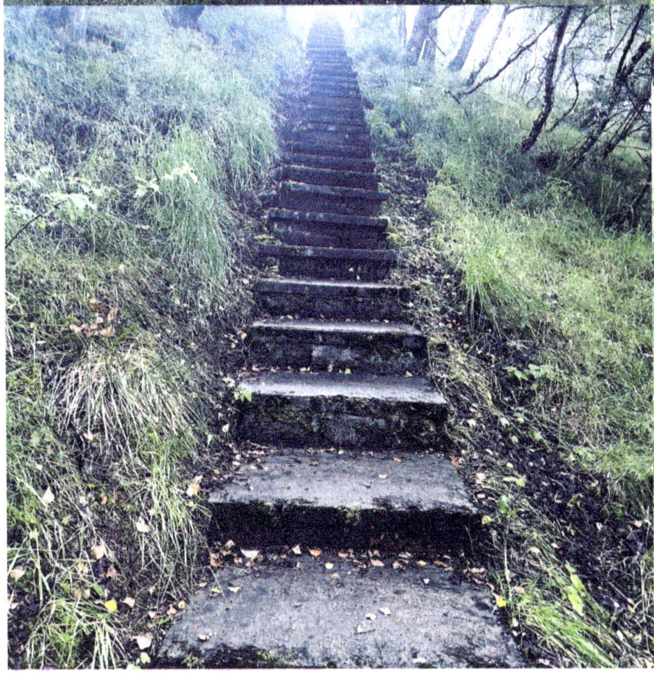

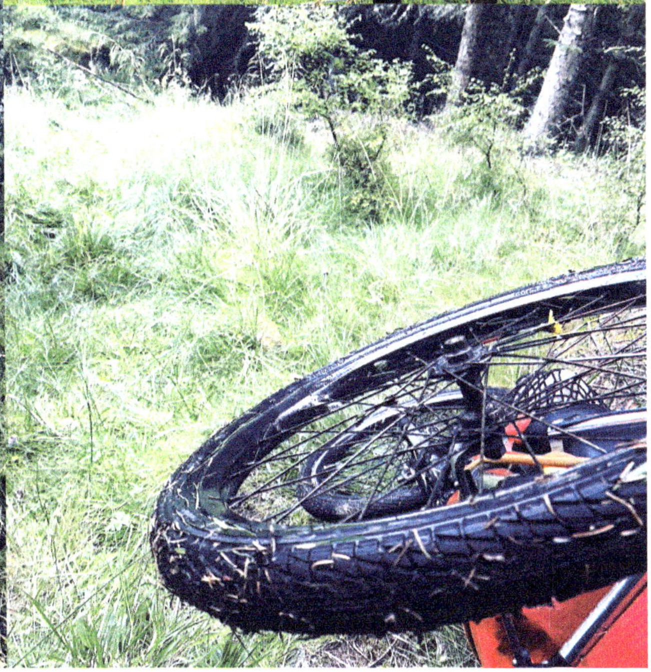

background and the sun low in the sky. After I crossed the bridge, I met a fellow 'End to Ender' on a bike. This lady was cycling north to south, the same direction as me, and we chatted for a while about our plans and how much harder the busy roads and weather were making things for us.

Meeting others doing the same challenge (I only met cyclists; nobody else was stupid enough to run it) would be one of the highlights of my day, as they were kindred spirits that completely understood what I was going through. Our conversations would sometimes only last a few minutes but would always leave me smiling and feeling more positive than five minutes beforehand.

It started to rain as I continued through the city, so I had my hood up and my head down. Whilst I was running down the side of a dual carriageway, someone called out from a car stuck in the traffic. I looked up to see my good friend Martin Curran, who has completed a lot of my extreme triathlons and was the first ever Scot to finish a 1x10 Deca. Once he was out of the jam, he found me again and we chatted for a while. Martin always makes me laugh and after my stressful day, it was wonderful to see a familiar face and be able to vent to someone.

After Martin left, I pushed on through the rain as the afternoon moved into evening. But the day hadn't finished with me yet. More verge walking and more swearing as the A9 continued. At least there was less traffic as the evening drew in. The route suddenly showed a left turn off the dual carriageway and I breathed a sigh of relief - finally I would be away from the lorries and cars. Unfortunately, my relief was short-lived as I came to a very long set of narrow, concrete steps leading downwards. They were wet and covered in slippery moss, and I was immediately nervous and messaged basecamp. "Are you sure this is ok?" I asked Gavin. He confirmed that it was, so I started my decent, holding tightly to the handlebars of the buggy. The weight and length of the pushchair made it extremely hard to control and I was very aware that if I slipped or let go, the jogger would fall and most likely be smashed to pieces by the time it reached the bottom.

Finally, I got to the end of the steps and made my way across a difficult section of forest ground which continued downhill. Slipping and sliding, at times I had to wedge the front wheel of the buggy against trees, just to gain back some control. There was a lot of cursing and much amusement from the basecamp messenger group as I sent pictures and tried to explain what was happening. Another set of steps, this time even narrower, lead to more swearing and sweating. The steps took me to what seemed like the bottom of the gulley, with no obvious way out.

I checked my position on my phone as I could hear water, but not see it. GoogleMaps showed that I was close, but between me and the bridge I needed to cross was a large area of thick mud. I stopped and looked at the bog, then back at the buggy. "Fuck" I said. I lifted the buggy over another tree root, and the Quiche which I had been saving for my evening meal fell into the mud. I picked it up and threw it as hard as I could. "FUUUUUUUCCCCKKKKK!!!!" I screamed into the trees.

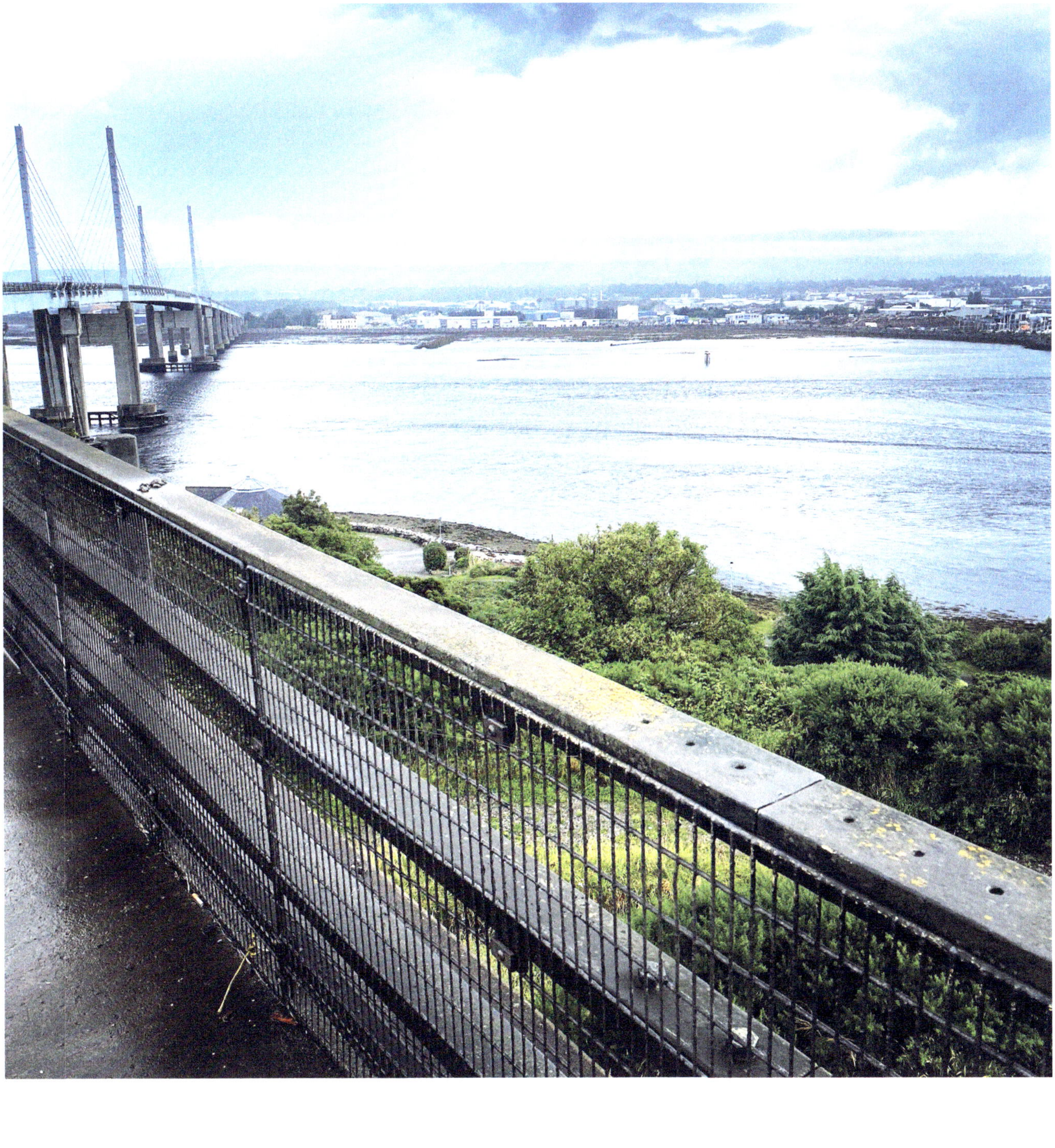

I took a moment.

This was one of those situations in life where you can (quite literally in this case) throw your toys out of the pram, play the victim, and generally behave like an idiot. But I was experienced enough at getting myself into trouble to know that losing your cool gets you absolutely nowhere. "Nobody is coming to rescue you, Claire" I said to myself "You need to make a decision and sort yourself out". By this point it was getting dark too, so I needed to decide on a course of action, fast.

I had no real idea how long the muddy section would go on for, or how the buggy would handle it. Would it get deeper? Would I get stuck? I decided it was best to go back the way I came as I knew that was doable. But there was no way I could get the buggy up the stairs pointing forwards, due to the size of the steps and length of the buggy. It would have to go backwards. With the buggy fully loaded, it was not only very hard to pull up the steep steps, but also risky. I would need to unload all the bags and take those up separately.

Once I had decided this, I got to work. The whole thing took me about 30 minutes, and I was hot and tired by the time everything was back to where I had started. I rolled my eyes and sighed with frustration but forced myself to look at the situation in a positive light. Yes, I had initially acted like a seven-year-old in a shopping centre, but once I had sorted my attitude out, I had made good of the situation.

I took a deep a breath and pushed back along the verge on the A9. I still needed to find somewhere to sleep, and it was now dark. Once I was off the A road and back on a quiet country lane (going uphill, obviously,) my options improved slightly, but a lot of the fields had locks on the gates and in the darkness it was harder to find somewhere to pitch my tent. I was so exhausted after my crazy day that when I saw a large open garden with an old derelict mobile home set off to one side, I decided that it would be perfect to sneak in and try to get some sleep.

Once my tent was up and water was boiling for some hot food, I thought back over the non-stop day I had just had. Hopefully tomorrow would be a little less crazy…

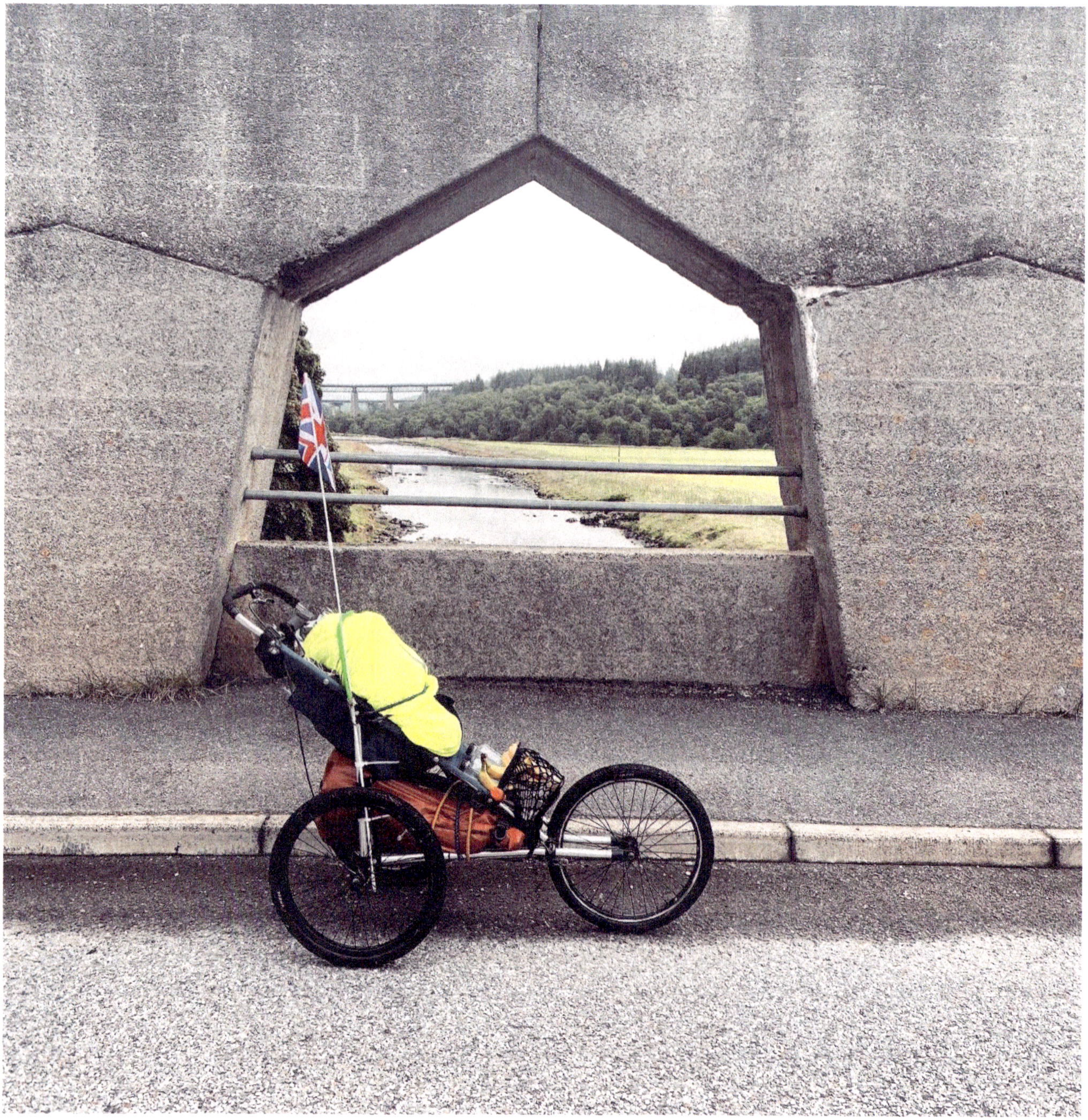

Day 4: Wednesday 19th August
Auchnahillin to Insh - 37.71 miles - Total mileage: 169.03

I lay in my sleeping bag, shivering. I looked at the clock on my phone - it was 3:30am. There was no point wasting anymore time trying to sleep, it just wasn't happening. I got up and inspected my feet. They weren't pretty, the blisters were really bad. I drained, cleaned and dressed them again, and found my trainers which were still soaked from the previous day's rain. My spare pair were dry, but as it was raining, I didn't want to use them yet. There was no point in putting on clean socks, either. I only carried a few pairs (I would be picking up fresh kit and supplies from a series of drop boxes that I'd posted to various locations along the route, prior to setting off). I pulled on last night's pair, saving the clean ones until the rain stopped and I was able to dry out my shoes.

I started packing everything down. The inside of my tent was wet with condensation and the outside with rain. I let out a sigh. I definitely didn't feel my normal happy, positive self this morning. Probably something to do with only eating a packet of Marmite flavoured crisps last night. I rolled my eyes and muttered "you're such an idiot" to myself.

I knew these kinds of challenges were rarely stopped by some big, dramatic event. More often than not, the accumulation of apparently insignificant errors and poor decisions are what lead to failure. Not eating enough, not drinking enough, not looking after your feet or general health. A blister left untreated can end a race. Not replenishing calories can lead to a deficit so great you don't have the energy to continue. I knew I must eat more, but I was finding it really hard to force down enough nutrition.

After a few hours of grinding up hills and running flat sections when possible, the sun started to rise. The views that surrounded me were amazing, vast fields and forests, shrouded in the early morning mist. The road was quiet, the only living things awake were me and the livestock. I munched on a block of Red Leicester for breakfast and listened to an Audiobook. My mood was lifting after the morning's grumpy start.

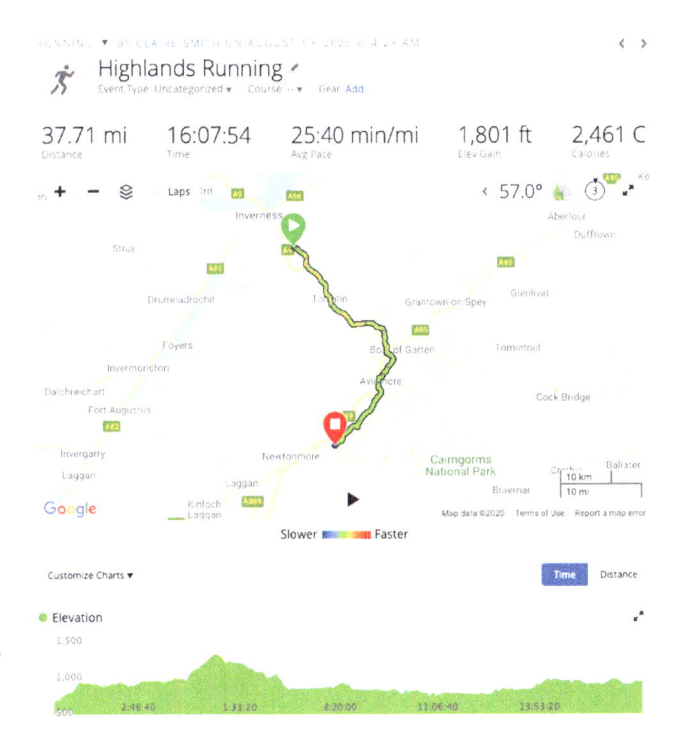

Unfortunately, as the morning went on negative thoughts began to creep in. By lunchtime I was starting to feel overwhelmed again by the challenge that lay ahead. Realising that I still hadn't really eaten anything substantial, I stopped in a village on a patch of grass and pulled out my stove to prepare a hot meal. Whilst my food cooked, I lay on the ground with my feet resting on a tree. I sighed with relief as the pain receded from my legs and the throbbing eased.

Being self-supported means you have to do everything for yourself. I'm fine with this, as I'm very independent and used to it. But that morning I missed having a crew. Someone who would know that I hadn't eaten enough and needed to get some decent calories in. Someone who could dry my soaking wet kit. And someone whose only focus was to help me move forward as fast and easily as possible. But that someone wasn't there and missing them only made me feel worse.

After my meal, I cracked on with getting some miles under my belt. The road was wide and quiet, and I enjoyed making some decent progress. That was until I hit another B road and things got serious again.

This particular road had no hard shoulder at all. A steep, narrow verge butted right up against it, making it impossible to get off the road if I needed to in a hurry. The traffic was busy and fast. And I was definitely in the way.

At one point someone had to do an emergency stop when another vehicle overtook me going in the opposite direction. Then I looked round to see a huge lorry speeding towards me and a large tanker close on the other side of the road. I quickly realised that they would pass me at the same time, so I tried to pull the buggy onto the verge to avoid being crushed.

I couldn't get out of the way quick enough - the lorry had to slam on the brakes to avoid hitting me or the tanker. It was a horrible moment; I could have been killed. I decided there and then that I could not, and would not, do this anymore. I made my way shakily back to where I started on the B road and pushed the jogger into a lay-by. I sat on some railway sleepers and put my head in my hands. I was only on Day 4. I had miles and miles of this to go, and I was sure that as I travelled further down the country, traffic was only going to get worse. As tears rolled down my face, I wondered if I simply wasn't going to be able to complete this brutal challenge I had set myself. I thought about all the people watching and supporting me, and the money I was raising for the hospice. I thought about Susan.

"No, fuck this." I said out loud. I can't give up. I pulled my phone from the top of the buggy and called my friend Matthew. Tearfully I explained what had just happened and my fears of having to abort. "Ok, then you have to change the route" he said, simply. We discussed my priorities. The record for fastest self-supported time, which had been weighing heavily on my shoulders, was relegated to last place. My first priority was now getting home

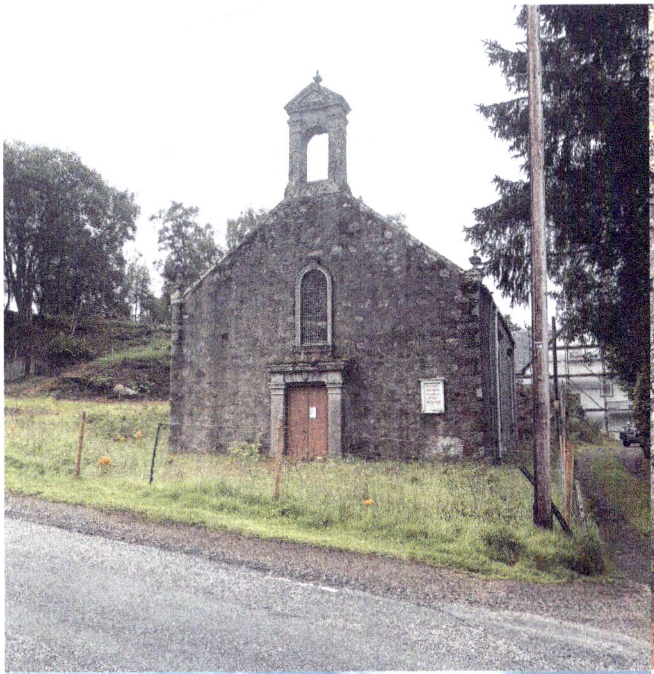
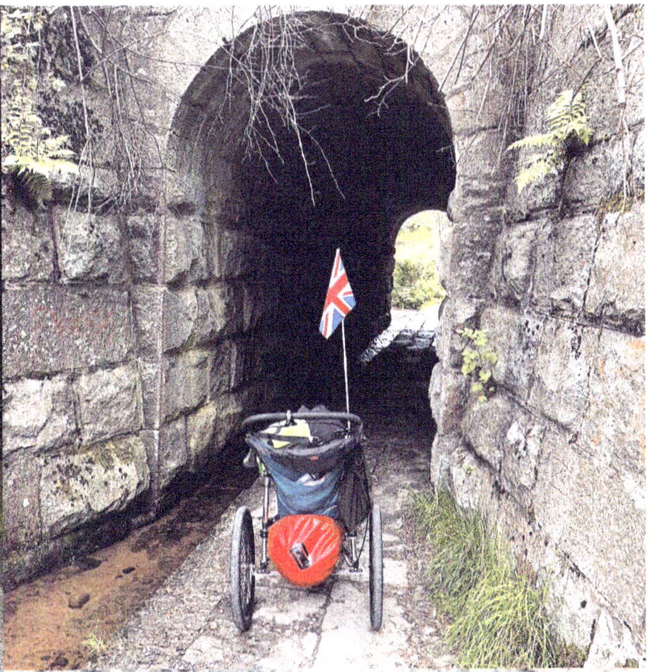
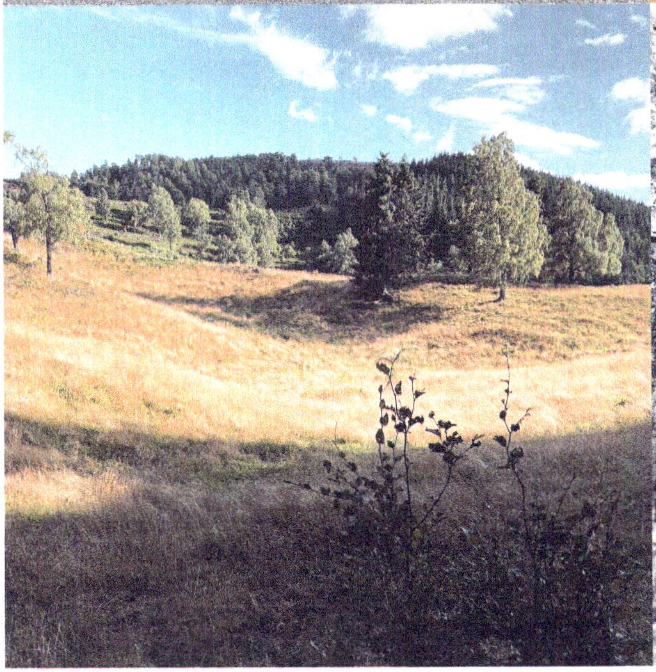
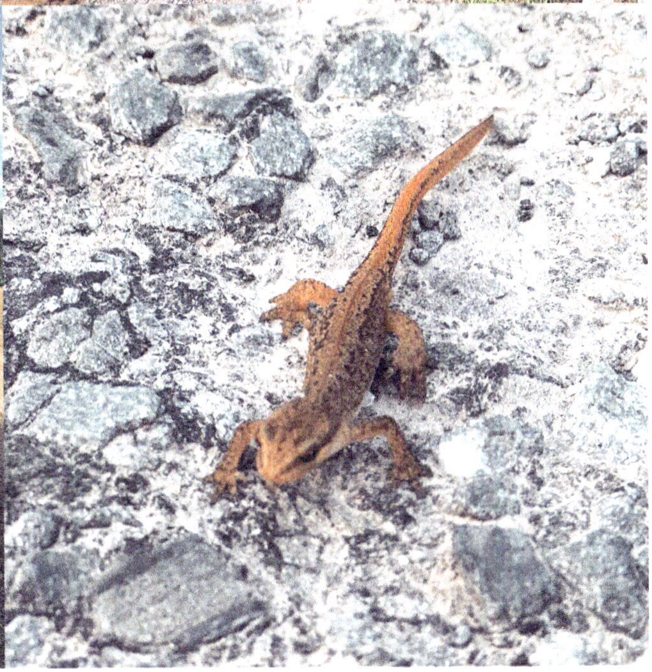

safely. Second priority, get to Land's End. I would give it my best effort; if I got the record, great, if not, so be it. It definitely wasn't worth dying for.

After chatting a while and feeling a little better, I messaged basecamp and explained the situation. Gavin was prepared, and within a few minutes sent over GPX files for an alternative route on a cycle path. I had to accept that my Brutal JOGLE was not going to be following the world record route. I would have to take less direct roads, which meant running further and inevitably taking more time to finish. But at least I wouldn't end up as roadkill.

My new route was on a rather nice gravel bike path and I made my way along it in the sunshine. I had accepted the fact that I would be doing more miles and probably more elevation too, but it also meant I could still push on with the challenge and for that I was grateful. The cycle path took me to a small village where I popped into a shop to get some supplies and treated myself to an ice cream.

The rest of the day passed uneventfully. It was super-hot, and I even saw a lizard on the road at one point which made me very happy. The heat also dried out my wet shoes which I had attached to the top of the buggy.

As the sun started to set, I began to look for a suitable place to put up my tent. The last couple of nights I had camped on sloping ground; far from ideal, as my sleeping bag would slide off the slippery mat and I would end up in a corner of the tent on hard ground. I walked past a gateway that led to a farmer's field. I thought for a moment, and then went back to look again. It seemed perfect. There was a small area of flat ground surrounded by a bank. I could see some farmhouses way off, but they shouldn't be able to see me.

I opened the gate, feeling a little like I was breaking in, and walked to the area I intended to camp. There were sheep around, but this didn't bother me. I decided to risk it and started putting up the tent. Once everything was sorted, I crawled inside and zipped up the door. There's something about being inside a tent with the door closed that makes you feel very vulnerable. It was still a little light outside and as I sat in the tent, inspecting my feet, I heard a car stop at the gate. I held my breath and waited. After a while they drove off. Was that the farmer? Were they now going to come over to make me leave? "Shit, why did I camp here", I said to myself, wishing it was dark already.

I was exhausted; the thought of having to pack everything away and find somewhere else to sleep was almost too much. I decided that if anyone did find me, I would offer money in return for a night's camping. And if that didn't work, I could always burst into tears. With the pain in my feet and how tired I was, crying would be easy.

I lay there for 45 minutes as it grew dark, eventually realising that nobody knew or cared that I was there. I finally relaxed enough to fall asleep after yet another roller-coaster day.

Day 5: Thursday 20th August
Insh to Calvine - 37.71 miles - Total mileage: 206.74

I woke at about 3:30am and lay in my sleeping bag for a moment. I had made it through the night without a grumpy farmer moving me on, but I had been rudely awakened in the early hours with an asthma attack. My asthma is mild and normally doesn't bother me much, but during the really tough endurance events that I have done in the past it's been a problem at night. I wake up gasping for breath and fumbling around for my inhaler. It's not a lot of fun, and last night I had been thinking, "I'm in the middle of nowhere and I'm going to die in a field of sheep". Then I remembered my GPS tracker, and that literally anyone with an internet connection could know where I am.

I packed down and quietly closed the gate behind me as I left. I loved the early mornings. The roads are quiet, and my energy levels are high. I ran the first 10 miles easily and felt like I was making progress. That morning was very windy but at least it wasn't raining yet. As I ran along, I amused myself with a game I called Frog or Stick. There were a lot of squashed frogs on the road, some of them in a bad way, and I tried to tell the difference between them and the twigs and sticks also in the road. It was not the best game I've ever played to be honest, but distraction is what we are really talking about here.

I passed through a town called Kingussie and wished there was a café open, as I was really craving fried bread (the rest of a cooked breakfast would be nice too). But it was early, so I made do with a Co-Op and stocked up on supplies. As I continued down the road, happily munching on a punnet of Strawberries, I thought about how little things make me happy during these crazy challenges. Finding a good food shop, seeing random supporters, or when the sun comes out.

After passing through a few villages and along a B road, I found myself at a large rocky monument on which someone has spray painted 'Cycle Path to Perth'. The path ran alongside the A9 and made me very happy, despite the 35mph headwind. I was on this all day, which meant no drama with traffic. All I had to do was keep

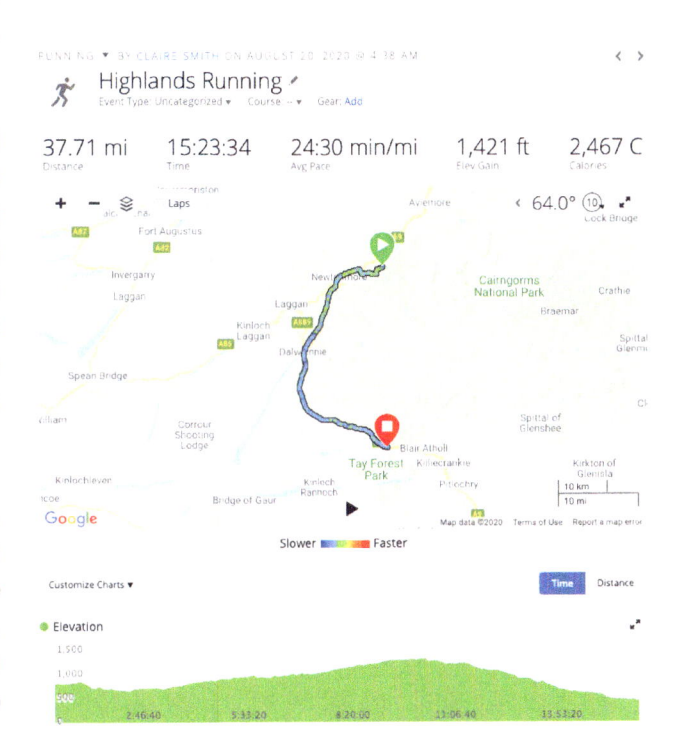

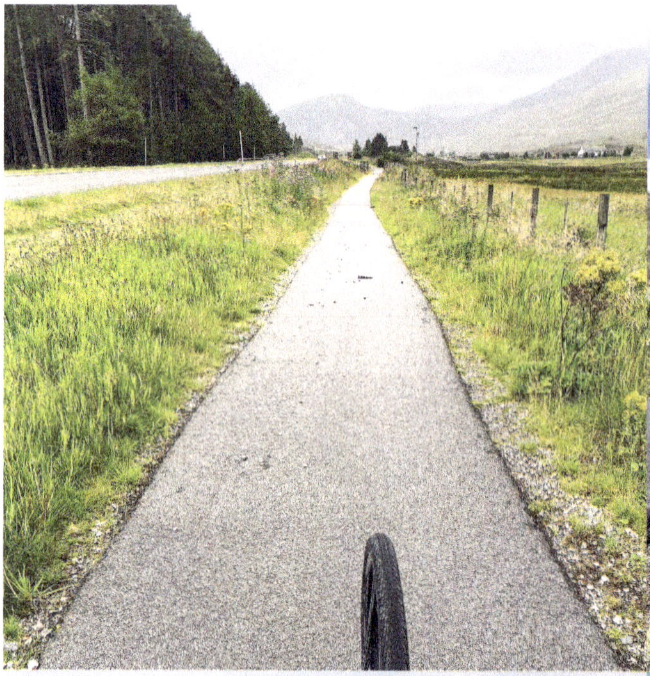
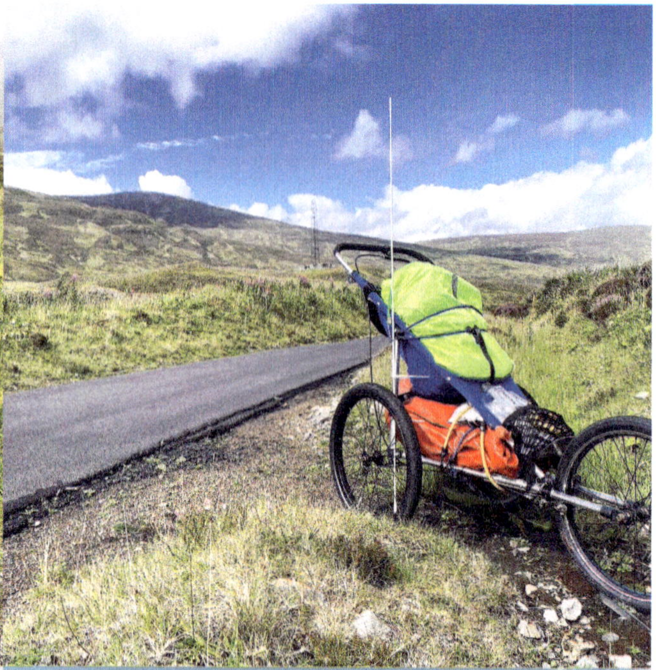
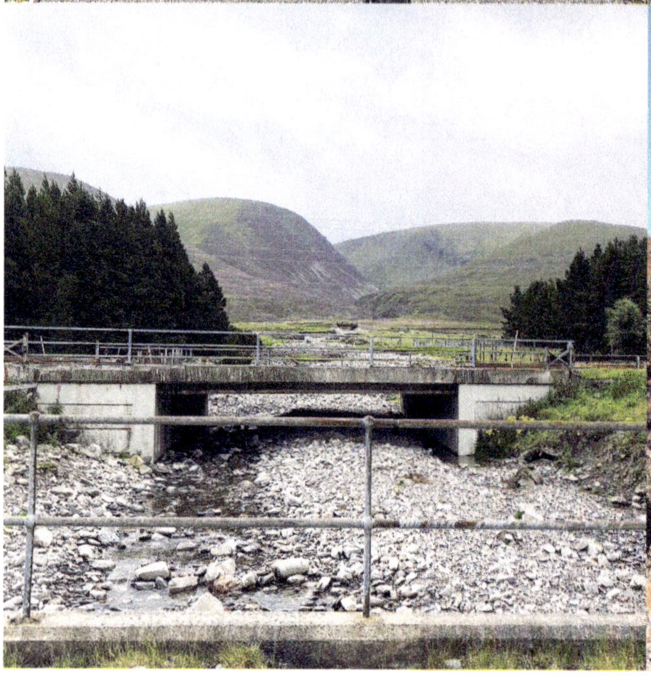
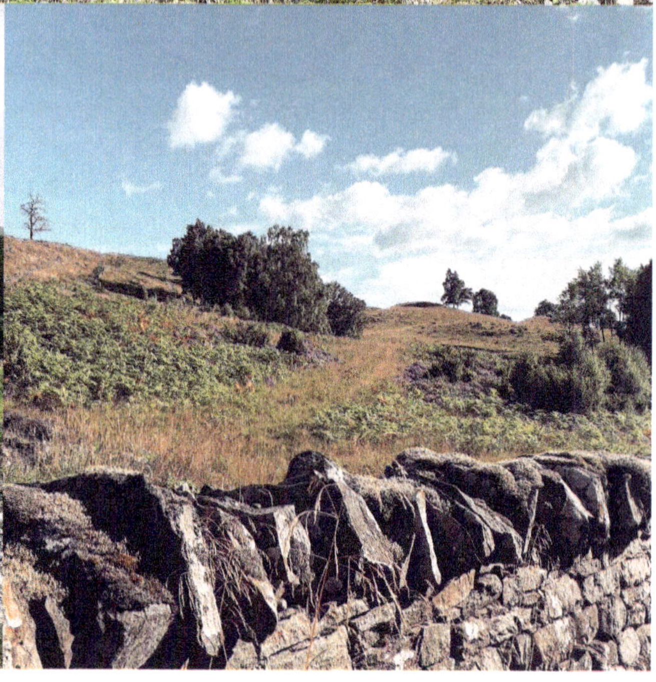

moving forward, so I put my head down and pushed on. There was no point trying to run into the wind as it was a struggle just to walk fast.

My feet were giving me a lot of issues today. My blisters were very bad now and the pain on the soles was intense to say the least. After about 20 miles, the only way I could manage the pain was by stopping every 5 miles to pull off my trainers and massage my throbbing feet. The feeling was beyond bliss and was (sadly) one of the highlights of my day. I couldn't stop for too long though, as the pain just got worse as the hours passed so the sooner I could stop properly and lie down, the better.

At some point I heard the sound of a helicopter over the A9 and looked up to see the coastguard approaching. As the helicopter passed I waved, and to my surprise and delight, the crew waved madly back at me. I was a little confused, but it made me inexplicably happy and I was now grinning like a seven-year-old. The helicopter flew away and I was on my own again, but minutes later they returned and waved again. This time I managed to record a short film as it was definitely a highlight, even beating the foot rubs. Later that night, I saw on Instagram that one of the crew had been following my journey and they were training in the area. He had messaged me to let me know that they would be trying to find me and say hello. It was a wonderful gesture and really picked me up. It's moments like that which made all the suffering worthwhile.

The day turned into evening and the bike path into a quiet, country road alongside fields and a river. I chatted to livestock and listened to an audiobook. Even though my feet were incredibly painful, I was quite content. At 37 miles I began to look for a good place to camp. It was limited though. A rough, wooded area to my right and a flatter, but more open, area to my left. But as the path ended and I approached the village of Calvine, I realised that I needed to make the best of it and that I wasn't going to be hidden away tonight. While I was setting up camp, a car full of young lads passed me. They all stared, and I pretended I hadn't seen their incredibly bright orange and loud Ford Focus racing past. I hoped that when they came back later on, they didn't decide to put the jogger in a tree for fun or something equally stupid. I attached the front wheel of the jogger to the tent so that at least I would get a heads up, but they had better things to do and that was the last I saw of them. Other than having to kill 8000 midges that had managed to get into my tent during the split second I opened the door, my night was uneventful.

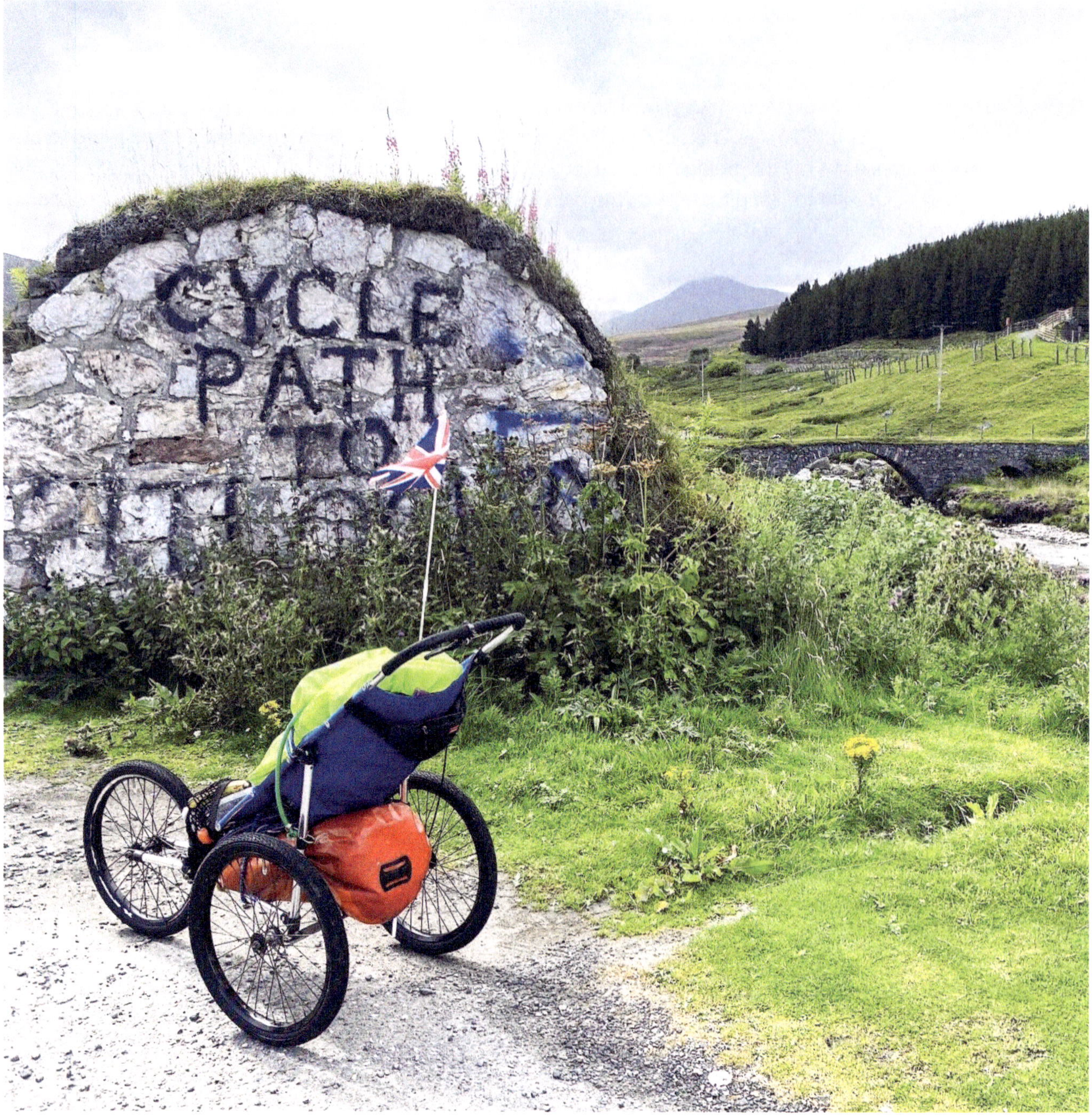
CYCLE
PATH
TO

Day 6: Fri 21st August
Calvine to Moneydie - 37 miles - Total mileage: 243.74

Today it seemed that my feet had had enough, and they were sick of dropping little hints. That morning they were screaming at me, and quite frankly looked an absolute state. I would lance, drain and clean my blisters at every opportunity, covering them with medicated talc afterwards. But with the almost constant rain, it was impossible to keep them dry. There was nothing I could do but swallow some pain killers and crack on.

Another early start meant I made it to Pitlochry as the shops opened, so I treated myself to a latte and Greggs sausage roll. As I waited for my coffee, a message came through from basecamp warning me that I needed to prepare myself for a new route that would be longer and harder. This confused me a little as I already knew this information… did they mean it was going to be even longer and even harder? Would I make it home for Christmas?

Once I had my drink, I sat in a small park eating my sausage roll with tears sliding down my face. Why did I ever think I could do this? At that moment I honestly thought there was no way in hell I could finish. Why had I even started? And what would people think if I gave up? More tears filled my eyes, and I didn't even bother to brush them away. Nobody was looking anyway.

I pushed on through the morning, but I couldn't shake off my negativity. Tears kept welling up in my eyes and despite telling myself to harden up, I just felt broken. More rain. More tears.

However, whilst climbing up yet another massive hill with rain dripping down my back and tractors trying to run me over, I saw a couple waiting on a verge at the top of the road. They waved at me and as I got closer, and I could hear them cheering and clapping. I was in the middle of nowhere and they had sought me out to say well done and keep going. Five minutes later I left them with a smile on my face, and my mood much improved.

Not long after, I met a Fireman called Sam (I don't think he was winding me up) who was cycling from Land's End to John o' Groats. We stood in the pouring rain, laughing and chatting about how we were getting on and when we hoped to finish.

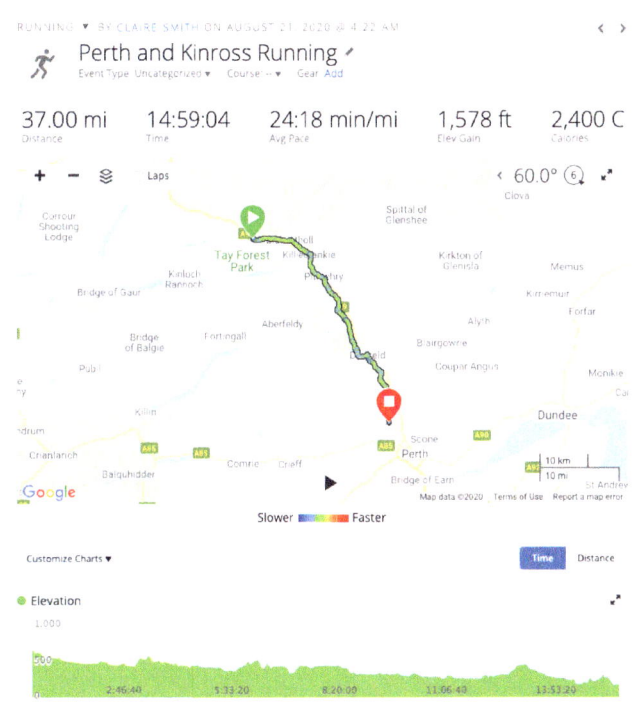

These small encounters with people (be it supporters or other adventurers) became a frequent part of my day and they were a source of energy to me. Like a can of Red Bull in human form, they would give me a buzz that lasted long after we parted. I had not really experienced this before, but I loved it and almost began to rely on it.

Feeling much better, I decided to stop for lunch. It was still raining, even harder now, so I invested some time in trying to find a deserted barn or something similar to shelter in. I eventually saw a pergola set in some very nice grounds of a posh estate, so I peered in through the open gates and wondered if I could skulk across to the pergola without anyone noticing. I decided it was worth the risk and pushed the buggy across the grass, leaving some very unsubtle tracks behind me.

Once I had made it to the shelter (scaring a pheasant who was also hiding from the rain), I sat down and munched on chicken sandwiches. I need to watch my mood, I thought. Staying positive whilst things were easy-ish and the sun shone wasn't too hard, but throw in some torrential rain, big hills and the thought that I might never make it to Cornwall, and it became very challenging.

"Ok, you've had a shit morning" I said to myself, "now you need to stop blubbing and feeling sorry for yourself. You need to push on and get this done".

Feeling better after a rest and some food, I got more miles in. The rain eased up, too. But having become so wet and cold, I soon felt exhausted again and by 2:00pm couldn't keep my eyes open. I was walking along the side of a river and saw a fisherman's club hut with a large porch area. As with most places it was closed due to COVID-19, but I didn't think it would be a major problem if I stopped there for a while. I pulled out my tent, and not even bothering with poles, crawled inside for 45 minutes of solid sleep.

The power nap helped enormously. For the rest of the afternoon my speed picked up and I felt a lot happier. Later as evening drew in, I started the nightly routine of looking for a good place to sleep. A few fields looked promising, but I kept on moving until I came across an outbuilding. As I looked at it, the thought of being undercover was very tempting. I walked down the drive a short way and saw a large house that the shed obviously belonged to. It was about 9:00pm. I hoped the occupants wouldn't put the bins out this late. Would they care or even know if I was there?

I decided to risk it, so squeezed the tent alongside the rubbish and bins. By the time I was set up it was dark, and I felt more relaxed. Boiling up some water, I made a curry flavoured Pot Noodle which tasted amazing after another tough day. As I settled down to sleep, I thought about the next day. I would get to Perth, then onwards to Edinburgh. If I could make it that far, finishing the Scottish leg of this challenge would start to feel like a real possibility.

HEIGHT OF FLOOD
1993
HEIGHT OF FLOOD
HEIGHT OF FLOOD
7TH OCT 1847
HEIGHT OF
FLOOD 1894.
HEIGHT OF FLOOD
5TH FEB. 1990.
HEIGHT OF FLOOD
15TH JUNE 1931
XVIII

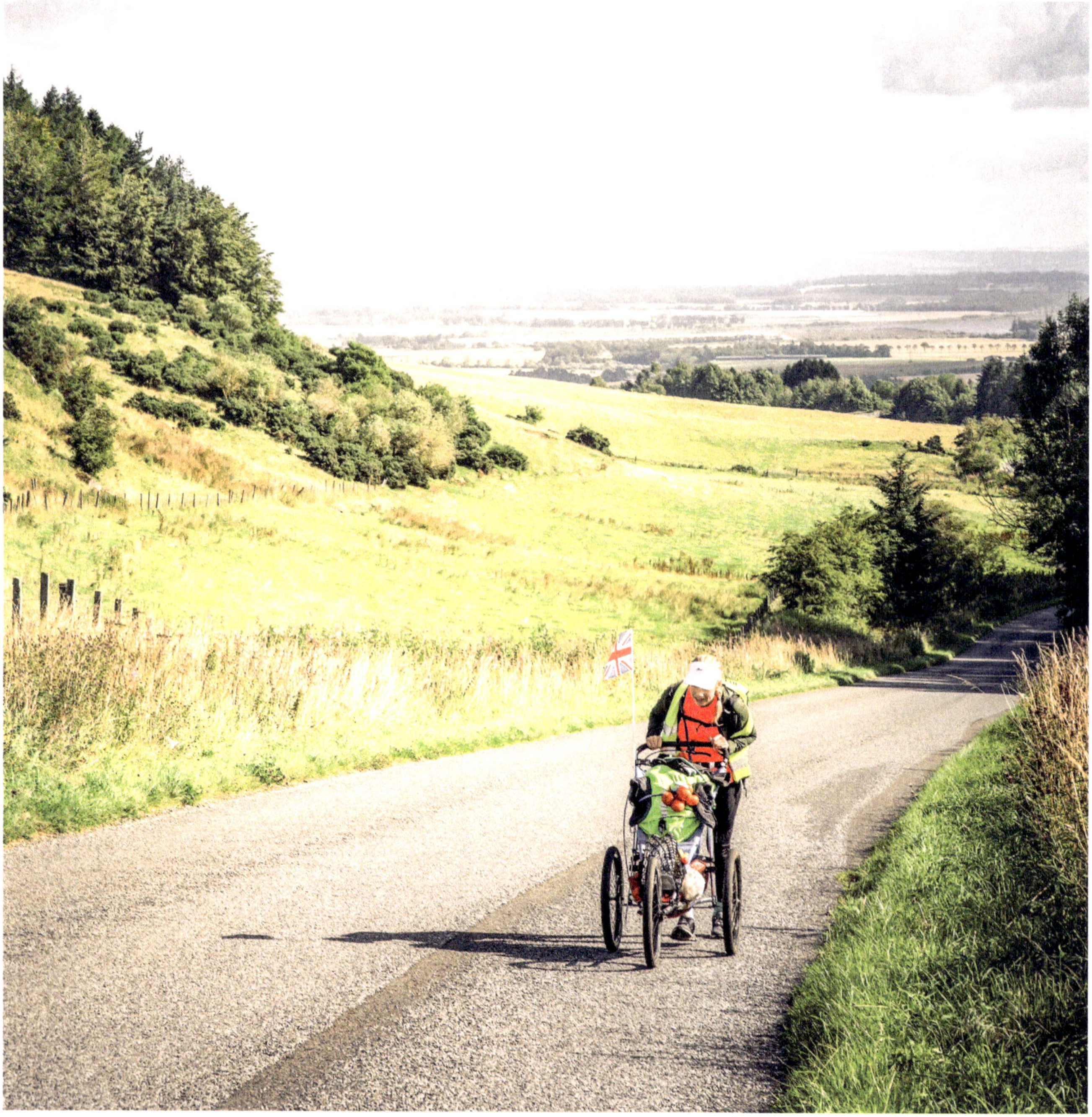

Day 7: Saturday 22nd August
Moneydie to Queensferry (Forth Bridge) - 41.11 miles - Total mileage: 284.85

I woke up after a really good sleep. The difference with being inside (even though the shed had no doors and I was *practically* outside) was immense. I worried that a crusty old outbuilding has become my dream house and that maybe this was a little concerning. Before setting off, I spent a little longer than normal having a 'wash' (baby wipes) and brushed my hair for the first time in a while. With all the wind and rain, it had become a giant dreadlock protruding from the back of my visor.

People had been talking about my DHB visor on social media and I feel it deserves a mention. I love my visor, and I'm not just saying this because I'm sponsored by DHB. It fits perfectly (doesn't give me a headache or fall off) and keeps my hair and the weather off my face. I can also hide behind it when I'm feeling rubbish. How was it still so white? Because it was on my head 90% of the time.

Feeling better once I was a little cleaner (note: do not take on self-supported challenges if you are unwilling to accept a significant drop in your standards of personal hygiene) I had a quick look in the mirror. Holy shit, what had happened to my face? My eyes looked like I'd been wearing goggles for a really long time. I quickly put the little mirror away and wonder why I had brought it at all.

As with every morning and night, my feet got most of the attention. My little toe was infected. That's a new issue, I said to the other toes. They didn't say anything back because they were all really pissed off with me. Red, sore, some oozing fluid. Even though I have a strong stomach, they still made me feel a little queasy. I cleaned them up as best as I could and apologised to them all.

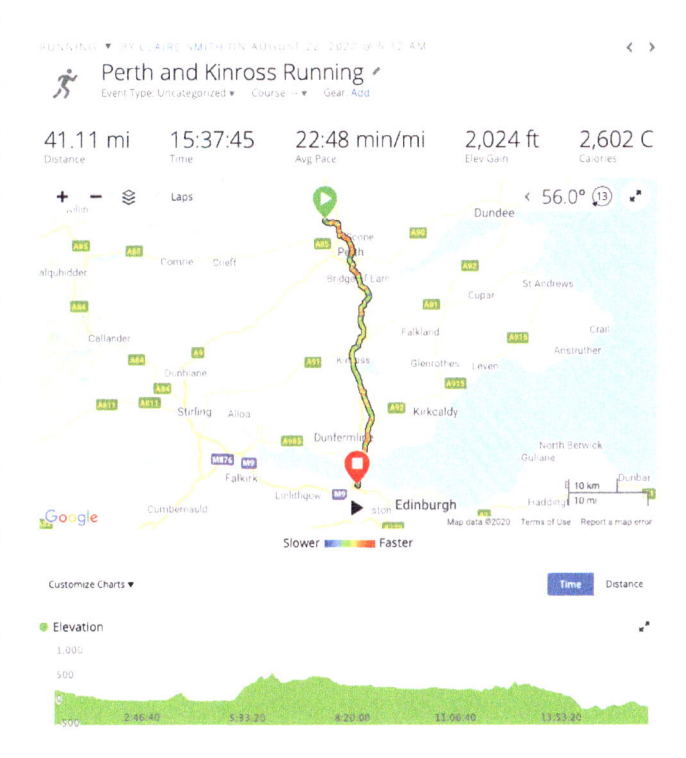

Once I had consumed my now regular breakfast of multiple painkillers, I was back on the road and on my way to Perth. I was low on food and water, so a restock was next on the agenda. The sun was shining and I felt good. The eight miles to Perth went by quickly. Once I was there, I found a supermarket and bought supplies. As well as the normal stuff, I treated myself to huge bag of mini-pastries for breakfast. Only when you are covering 40 miles a day on foot can you eat that amount of pastries and have them not even touch the sides.

Today a photographer called Carol was coming to find me on the road and take some images. The hills were relentless - after covering the first 10 miles in good time, the next 10 were ridiculously slow. Eventually I saw a lady waiting at the top of the road with a large camera and I thought to myself it was fitting most of her shots would be of me, head down, going slowly uphill.

After Carol left me, I had a short break with my feet up against a wall, trying to ease the throbbing a little. The good mood of the morning was disappearing fast, despite desperately trying to hold on to it. I sat up and stared to pack things away and get moving again. After a few minutes, a woman who passed me that morning in her car while shouting encouragement out of the window, shows up again. My first thought was "Oh God, not someone else." Not because I don't like meeting people, but I was in a lot of pain by that point and I found it so hard to be upbeat and positive when my feet hurt that much. I'd also had quite a few visitors already that morning and really just wanted to be miserable on my own for a while.

Luckily, Ginny seem to pick up on this and became the perfect company for a few miles through the small town of Kinross. We shared the same values and sense of humour; she even took me to see her bike mechanic, who gave the jogger a check-up. As we sat waiting outside the bike shop, we chatted about previous long-distance triathlons we had completed and laughed about how we got through them. By the time Ginny left me, I felt 100% better. It's amazing how some people's energy can lift you up and help push you on.

The last thing Ginny and I had talked about was getting to 'The Bridges'. I have to be really honest here and disclose that most of the time during this challenge (and also in my day-to-day life) I don't really know where I am. My sense of direction is appalling, I don't know whether I'm facing north or heading south. If I was forced to admit it, I barely know my left from my right. Navigating has always been a challenge for me, and without Sat Nav or the GPS on my phone, I'm quite literally lost.

So, when these 'Bridges' were mentioned, I thought I'd better have a look at the map. It turned out that I was going to be crossing the Firth of Forth by one of three bridges called the Forth Bridge… I was quite confused by this, but Gavin at basecamp said it would be 'iconic', and they wanted to meet me there to take photos. I was still about 16 miles away and it was already early afternoon. "In that case I'd better get a move on" I said to myself. Unfortunately, my body had other ideas. Despite my newly found positive attitude, within a few miles my feet were screaming again, and I was suddenly overwhelmed with tiredness. Passing an empty car park containing a lonely monument and a shipping container, I decided this would be an ideal place to have an afternoon nap. Once again, I used my tent like a bivy bag to save time and crawled inside to sleep. 30 minutes and two pork pies later, I was a new woman and ready to get to The Bridges.

The next few hours passed rather pleasantly. The rolling hills and gorgeous views kept me entertained. I passed through villages, some clearly affluent and others less so. I found it interesting to compare how people lived such different lives when geographically they were not so far apart. It was also funny how people reacted to me, as with my loaded baby buggy and Hi-Viz jacket, I wasn't exactly subtle. As I went past one house with peeling paint and an over-grown garden, I saw an old man looking out of the window at me. He was very thin and wearing a large cowboy hat.

The next thing I knew, he was shouting after to me to stop. I turned and saw him shuffling towards me. "What are you doing?" he asked in a strong Scottish accent. As I explained, his eyes got bigger and his mouth hung open. "Well, good luck!" he said, then turned and went back to his house and shut the door. I laughed and started running again. Within 20 minutes of Cowboy Hat Man, a police car passed me and pulled into the lay-by just ahead. Once again, I explained what I was doing and the two policemen asked for selfies, called me crazy and wished me luck. I had so many of these types of interactions with everyday folk, just curious as to what I was doing. They always made me smile.

I pushed on. More hills. More views. As the afternoon turned into early evening, the surrounding area became more urban and I was finally rewarded with my first view of The Bridges. This gave me a huge boost and I picked up my pace a little. I was still unsure of whether I would actually cross the water tonight, or find somewhere to stay on the near shore. Finding somewhere to sleep in a town would be almost impossible, and I would certainly have an uneasy night with people (mainly drunk) wandering about. However, it was decided in the basecamp chat that I should go for it, which actually made things quite exciting. It felt like I was on a mission to cross a border, even though I was still a long way from actually doing that.

Once I made it to The Bridges, I understood why Ginny and Gavin had been so keen for me to get there. They were pretty impressive, each bridge being constructed in a completely different architectural style and built in a different time period. I was also really pleased I was crossing the firth at night. It was quieter, and the lights, especially from the Queensferry Crossing, were absolutely stunning. I was buzzing.

That was until I got to the entrance of a massive 'East footway/cycle track closed' sign that stood in front of me: Please use the stairs to access the north footway/cycle track. "Ah. Just use the stairs," I said to the sign. "Do you

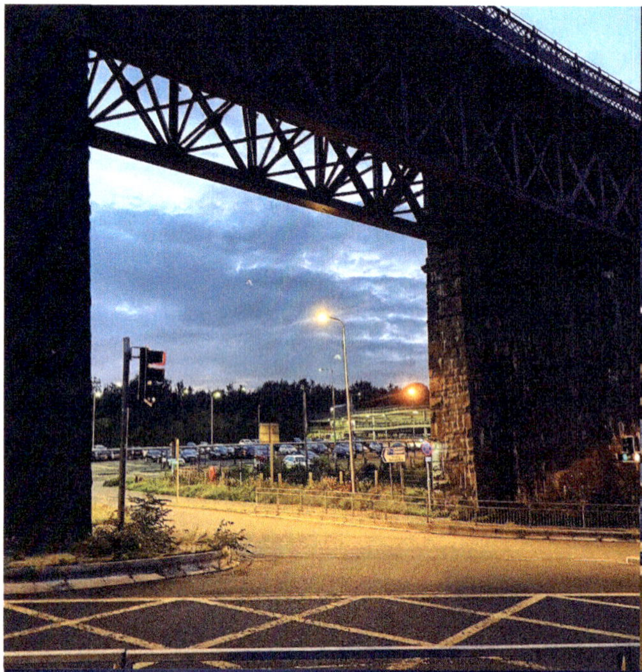
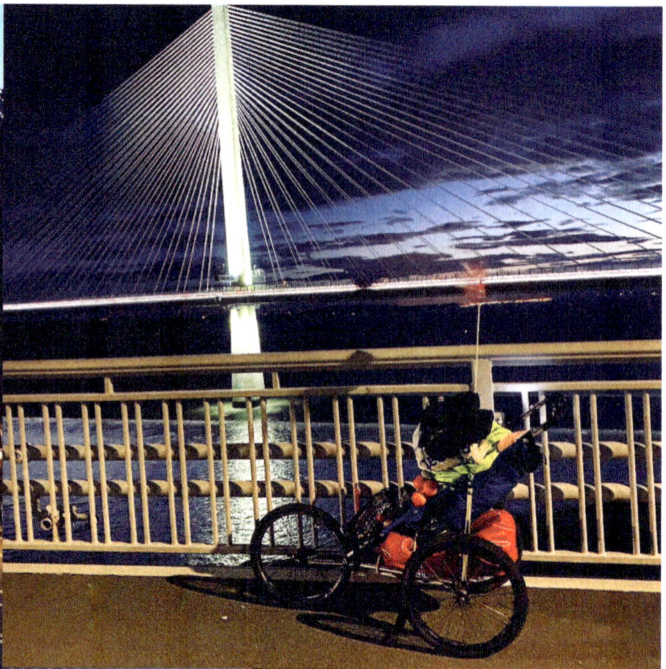
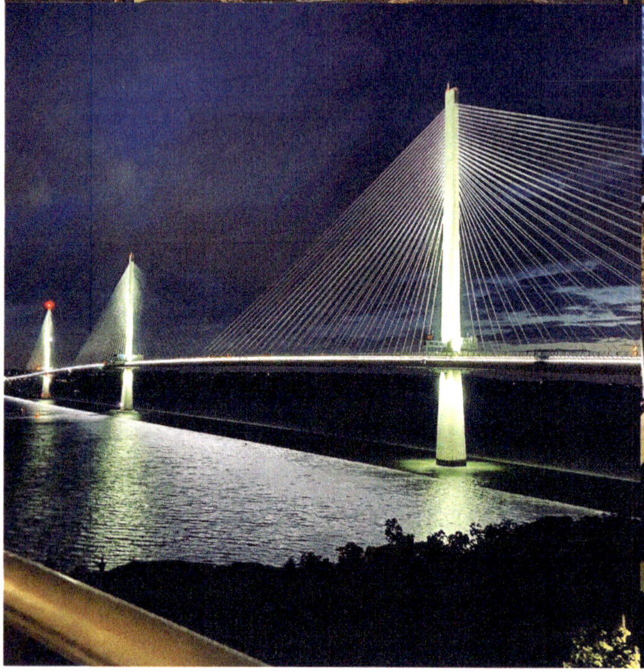
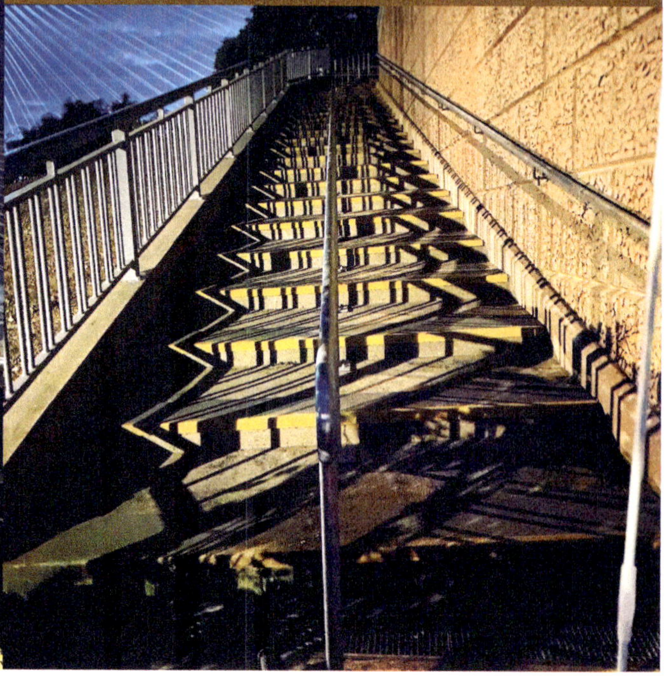

know how difficult it is to 'use the stairs' with this bloody buggy?" The sign did not offer any helpful suggestions, so I gritted my teeth and set off to find the steps.

Standing above a steep, seemingly endless set of stairs leading downwards, I had a flashback to what felt like weeks ago (but was actually only four days) of me struggling to hold on to the heavy jogger whilst it pulled me down into a ravine. At least I knew what to expect. Holding on tightly to the handlebar with one hand and the rail with the other, I braced myself to start the descent. It wasn't as difficult as the time before, the steps were dry and not covered in slippery moss for a start, but it was still stressful. One mistake could send the buggy flying down, smashing into pieces at the bottom and ending my JOGLE attempt. I tried not to think about it and just concentrated on one step at a time. Once I'd got to the bottom, I was faced with yet another set of steps and finally a flight leading upwards.

When I made it to the north foot path, I breathed a massive sigh of relief. I looked around me and instantly forgot about my struggles as the view was breath taking. The lights from the Queensferry Bridge reflecting in the water to my right were quite something. With a huge smile plastered over my face, I started to cross the firth. Gavin was also somewhere on the bridge, waiting to meet me at the halfway point. I started to run, holding on to my visor in the strong wind (Gavin told me later that it was a 'mere breeze').

My eyes strained, desperately looking for people. Where were they? My Garmin bleeped at me; I was close to 40 miles, but the low battery warning was now showing. Aargh... not a good time to stop and rummage around for a spare right now. Deciding to risk it, I pushed on. Finally, I saw three silhouettes in the distance. They waved at me, I waved back madly, and tried to run a little faster.

Gavin, his wife Mido, and their daughter joined me, and we all chatted excitedly as we continued back the way they had come. When we were close to the end of the bridge, another person emerged from the shadows. He told me his name was Paul, and that he had been following my tracker and seen that I was crossing the Forth Bridge tonight. I desperately tried to recall a 'Paul' that had taken part in The Brutal Triathlons, as he seemed to know me. After a while he introduced himself to Gavin. I realised with absolute horror that he was my best friend's brother, Paul, son of Susan Northcott, the very reason we were all on that very bridge at 10:00pm on a Saturday night. I hoped he hadn't noticed my vagueness, or if he had, put it down to extreme tiredness. The fact that I hadn't actually seen Paul since he was about 12 didn't help me, but I was still very annoyed with myself.

Shortly after meeting up with Paul, a cyclist appeared who was clearly very excited about catching up with me. "I've been glued to your tracker and when I saw you were crossing the bridge tonight, I had to come and see you" he said, grinning widely. His name was John, and he had completed the Oner Ultra Trail Run a few years back. "Do you want to sleep in my front garden?" he asked. "I live literally the other side of the bridge." That was absolutely perfect, as both me and my Garmin were running out of energy.

Once we were all across the bridge, Gavin and his family offered Paul a lift home and we said our goodbyes. John and I walked the short distance to his house, and he showed me where I could pitch my little tent. After asking if I needed anything and taking a selfie with me, John went back into his house, leaving me alone again. I took a deep breath. Wow, what an amazing day that was. I pitched my tent and boiled some water for my Pot Noodle. Whilst I sorted my feet out, still smiling from everything that had just happened, I received a text from my son, Jake.

"You're doing great, mum" he said, "I'm so proud." My eyes filled with tears. My kids are so cool. They never judge me when I fail but are always so pleased for me when I do well. Jake then went on to tell me he was leaving home and moving into university accommodation before I would finish my JOGLE. I took a moment to process this information, unsure of how I felt about it. A little overwhelmed, definitely, but it was now my turn to be proud of my son who was making proper grown-up decisions in his life.

A few happy tears later, I threw some talc on my poor toes, practically inhaled my food, and settled down to sleep.

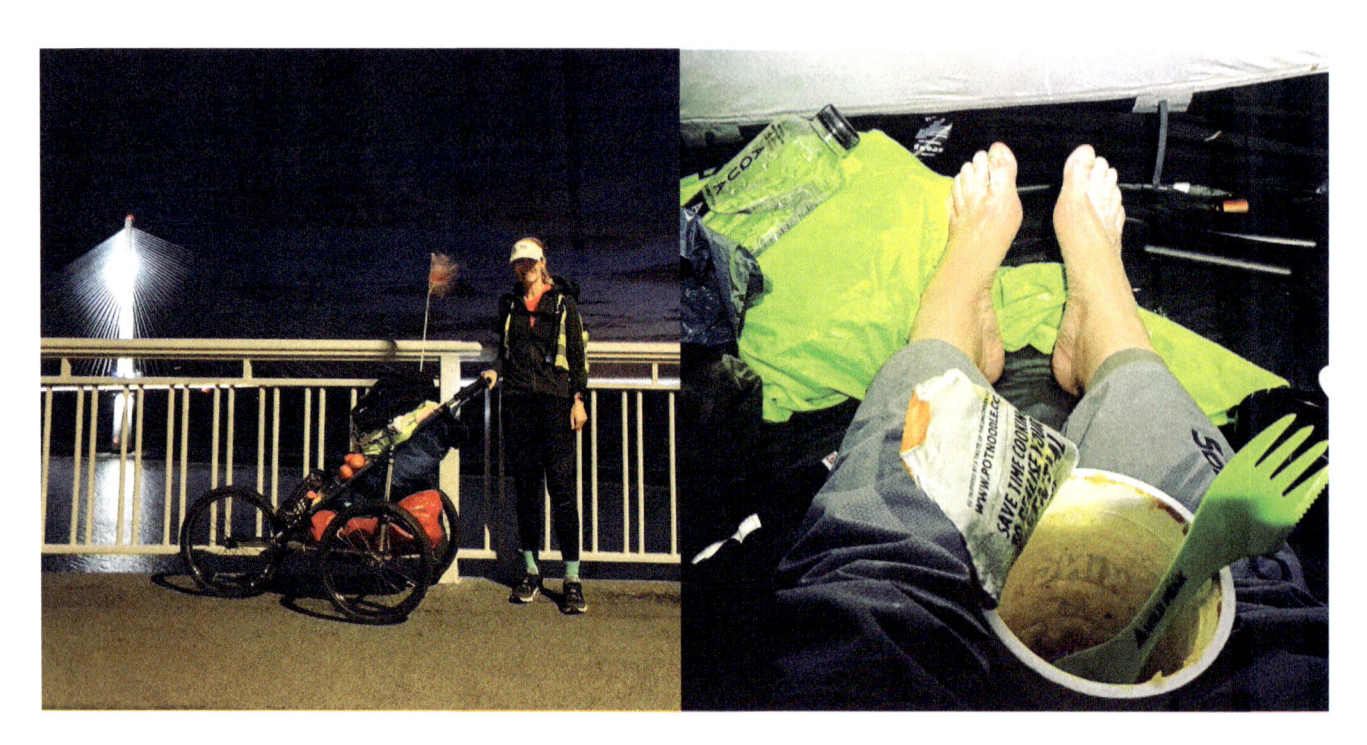

Day 8: Sunday 23rd August
Queensferry to West Linton - 23.36 miles - Total mileage: 308.21

I woke up and my first thought was that I had been on this crazy journey a whole week! The second thought was that I had no idea what I had coming to me when I started this challenge. Then I remembered the previous night, and that I was in someone's front garden. I got dressed, packed my tent down quietly, switched on my head torch and made my way across the park to the road.

I was feeling really tired; yesterday had been super-busy, with a later finish than normal so I could make it across the bridge. I didn't regret it, but I had a feeling I was going to pay for it today. After picking up some more food, I phoned Kathi for a chat. She was stretched out on her sofa, enjoying a relaxing Sunday morning. We talked for 45 minutes, laughing about all the mad things that had happened so far. I love Kathi, she's the sort of person you don't forget once you've met her. She is wonderfully kind and generous, with a wicked sense of humour too. I don't have to say much to Kathi either, she just gets me and whatever's going on at the time. I tell her about the previous night and how it had seemed wrong that she wasn't there with me and Gavin. But Brighton is a long way from Scotland, she reminded me.

After my chat with Kathi, my route took me through a golf course. It was still early but there were a few people about. I was on a small road which Gavin had assured me was a public right of way, but as an expensive car came towards me, I realised that the driver was going to deliberately force me into the verge. I glared at the driver as he passed and said, "good morning asshole," loud enough for him to hear me. He kept his eyes firmly forwards, not acknowledging me in any way. This was the first openly hostile encounter I had had on my JOGLE and it bothered me a little.

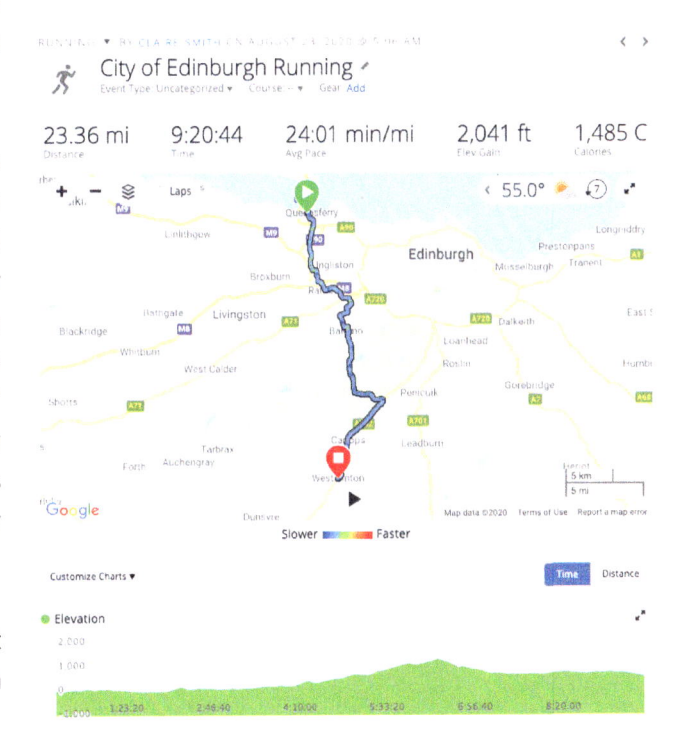

A few minutes down the road I stopped for a moment to adjust my dry bag, as it was starting to slip through the bungy cords that attach it to the jogger. I leant down to fix it, and once I was done, stood up again. There was another expensive car in front of me, with yet another miserable looking man behind the wheel. He muttered something I couldn't hear and waggled his hand at me to move. I pulled over to one side so he could pass, then stuck my middle finger up at him. Childish? Maybe, but I didn't care. Too much money can turn people into real idiots.

I tried to shake off the bad feeling the golfers had left me with by starting to run, but after a while I had to stop, breathless. I was completely exhausted. I was also a little apprehensive, as this morning I would be going over the Pentlands (a hilly, off-road section west of Edinburgh). How would the jogger hold up, I wondered? I wasn't too worried about going up the hills myself as I had been doing that for seven days now, but the downhills worried me.

About an hour later, Gavin and another Brutal Events friend, Richard, appeared. They didn't know each other prior to today but were soon chatting about the Double Brutal and which year they had completed their races. I love how The Brutal connects people, it makes all the event organisation red tape and hassle so worthwhile. Once Richard had said good luck and goodbye, Gavin turned to me. "You ready to take on the Pentlands?" I wasn't sure about ready, but I felt better that he was there.

"This is where I do a lot of my training" Gavin explained to me as we walked. "My playground, if you like." I looked around me. The heather gave the surrounding rugged ground an amazing purple hue. "It's beautiful" I said. He pointed out where we were heading. It didn't seem too high, so I relaxed a little. But as we chatted about The Brutal, the path started to get rougher, causing the jogger to start bumping and bouncing all over the place. I was starting to get anxious; the jogger was pretty robust, but it wasn't designed for going over such rough terrain whilst carrying the equivalent of a monster baby. I was worried that something would break, and then what would I do? I tried to take the smoothest path possible, but this was proper off-road stuff. There were a few sections where I struggled to push it up and over some large cracks and potholes in the ground.

Once we had made it to the top, there was just the downhill section to go. I prepared myself for the struggle of hanging on to the buggy whilst it desperately tried to make a bid for freedom. By the time we had crossed the Pentlands I was exhausted, but relieved that the section was over. I thought back to sitting in my kitchen at home, a few weeks before I left, looking at GoogleMaps and Gavin explaining that I needed a better route for the buggy. That seemed like a lifetime ago now.

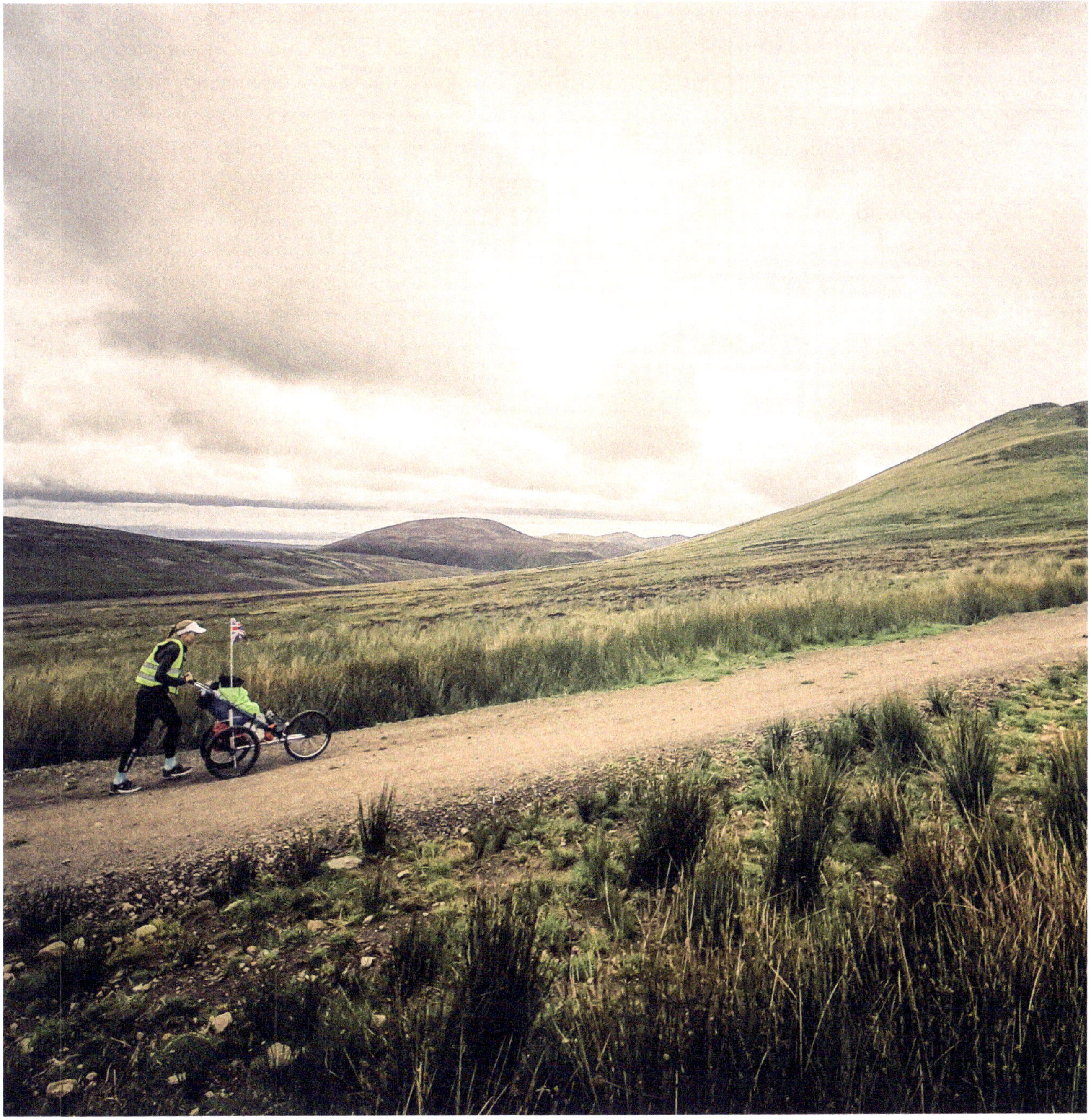

We got to the road and Gavin turned to me. "My house is about six miles from here, I'll see you soon," and with that he was gone. I was left standing with the jogger, a little confused. Six miles? I thought it was a lot closer than that. At that moment, six miles might as well be a 100. I set off down the road and was immediately faced with the choice of a narrow pavement covered in low, overhanging branches, or a very fast and busy road. The pavement soon became impossible to use due to the width of the jogger, so I was forced to fight it out with the traffic. The Sunday drivers were not impressed with me being in their way, and in my over-tired state, I became irrational and angry. My feet throbbed and I was now also experiencing shooting pains in my left Achilles.

A few tears rolled down my face, as self-pity welled up inside me. I tried to pull myself together, but I just felt awful. How had I gone from laughing with Gavin a minute ago, to crying in a road the next? This was all a part of the JOGLE rollercoaster ride that I was well and truly strapped into now. I just had to hang on and get through it.

By the time I made it to Gavin's house I was in bits. A few of Gavin's friend's in the village had stood at their gates to clap for me, but I think it was fairly obvious I wasn't in the best way. I tried to smile with conviction and wave at the children, but I was fooling nobody.

Gavin led me to his garden and offered me a seat on the patio. I immediately pulled off my trainers and socks and started rubbing my feet, which in hindsight was pretty rude and unpleasant for all concerned due to the horrific state of them. Luckily, endurance athletes understand this kind of stuff. A steaming mug of tea and another one filled with home-made leek and potato soup was placed in front of me and I had to fight back the tears of gratitude that sprang to my eyes. I am an emotional wreck today, I thought.

After tea, soup and sitting down had worked their magic, I began to feel better. But the thought of grabbing my drop-box (I had posted clean kit, dehydrated food and medical supplies to Gavin's house prior to starting the challenge) and hitting the road again made me want to start crying. What I really wanted was for Gavin to tell me to stop and have a shower, more hot food, and to sleep in a real bed. But he wasn't going to do that. I had to give *myself* permission to do that. I wrestled with this for a good hour before finally asking Gavin if I could stay the night. "Of course," he said. "You have a shower and I'll give the buggy a check-over".

As I climbed into the shower, I caught my foot on the tray. I had to put my hand over my mouth to muffle a howl of pain. My feet were absolutely ruined. Once I forced myself to get out of the shower, I looked at them properly now they were clean. "Good God," I muttered to myself, wondered how they would make it to Cornwall.

Gavin had been busy during my prolonged shower, fixing the jogger's front wheel which had been causing it to constantly pull to the left. He had also put some extra tape on the handlebars to provide more padding. As my hands were already covered in calluses, this would be a welcome relief. Another friend of mine had been waiting down the road to say hello. Susan arrived and without thinking about the social distancing rules we were supposed to be abiding by, gave me a massive (and much needed) hug, and told me how well I was doing. Once again, I had to bite my lip to hold back the tears. I explained to her that by stopping at Gavin's I had failed in some way. I had only managed 23 miles today and felt like I should still be on the road, wild camping again that night. Susan shook her head and told me I needed to rest up properly tonight.

After Susan left, I sat at the table with Gavin's lovely family and ate Macaroni Cheese pie. Although this is literally my idea of the perfect pie, I struggled to eat as my stomach felt off and I was so tired. I listened to the chatter from his girls about how they would be returning to school after lockdown, but all I wanted to do was sleep. After the meal, I finished sorting my kit and filled my water bottles so that the next morning I could just get up and go. I said goodnight to everyone and by 8:00pm I was curled up in a double bed, fast asleep.

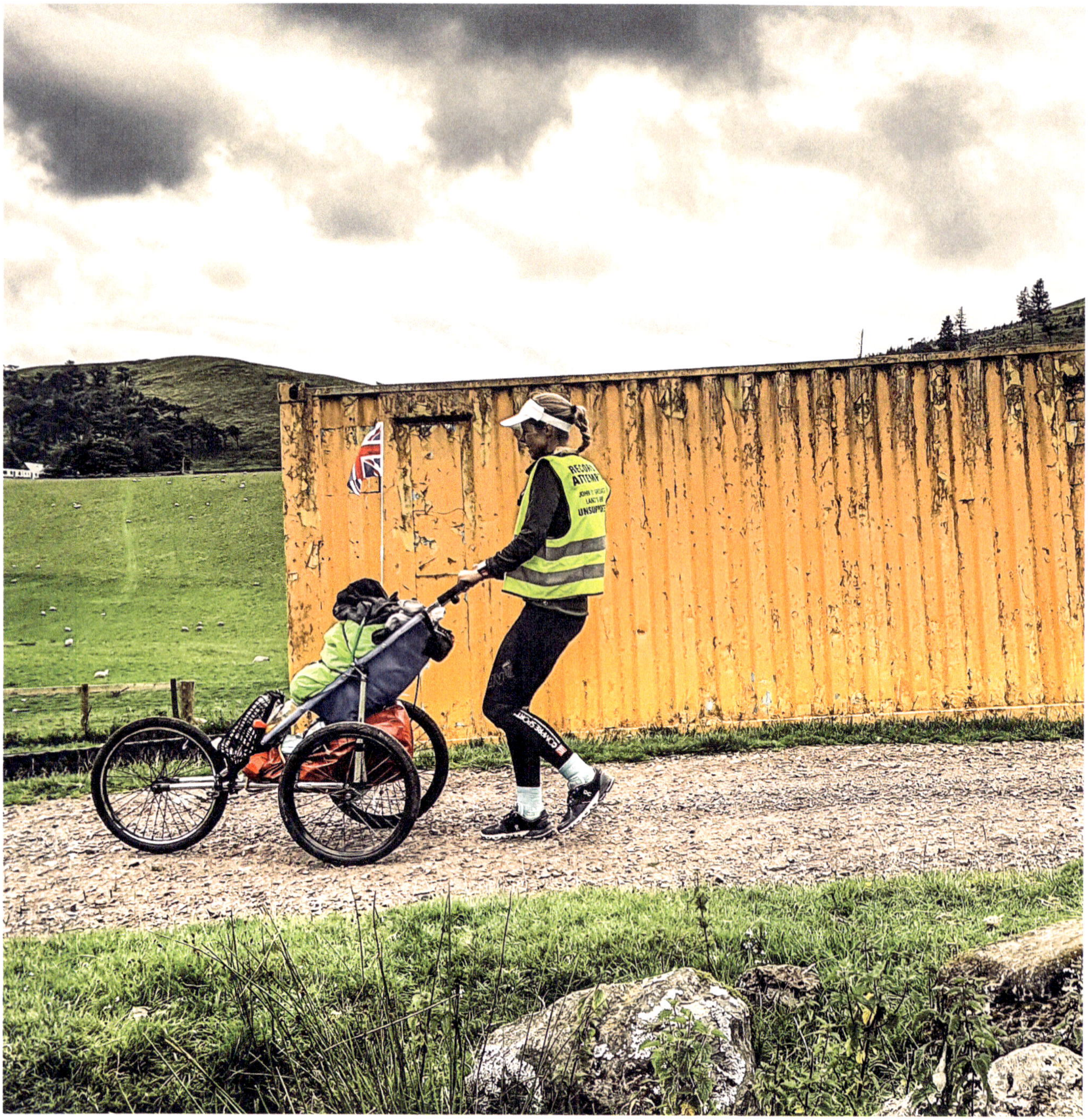

Day 9: Monday 24th August
West Linton to Beattock - 38.61 miles - Total mileage: 346.82

When I woke up at 5:00am, I didn't know where I was for a moment. I sat up blinking and looked around. This was definitely not my tent and I was not in a random field. I lay back down for a minute and briefly entertained the thought of going back to sleep, but I sat up sharply. What was I thinking? Pulling off the duvet, I had a shower and got myself ready to hit the road. I needed to get back to it as quickly as possible. I could feel myself weakening, wanting to go home, not wanting to leave Gavin's. Did he need a lodger, I wondered?

After two amazing coffees, Gavin walked me to the edge of the village. I was a little sad to leave him and as the rain got heavier, I felt a dark cloud hanging over me. After the high of crossing the Forth Bridge and the lovely break at Gavin's yesterday, my head was all over the place. I had a little chat with myself, going over all the reasons why I was doing this challenge, asking the surrounding sheep for their input (limited) and basically trying to get my mental state back to where it needed to be. While I was doing this, without realising it, I found myself on another off-road section. With all the recent rain, it was super-muddy. I checked my navigation app. I was on the right path, but it seemed to be a bit of a shortcut, the kind of shortcut I didn't want to take. The sort that generally caused the jogger issues. Eventually I found my way back to the road and started running. My Achilles was still hurting from yesterday and try as I might to ignore it, I was finding it hard. "Stay positive, remember" I muttered to myself. I'd had niggles from the start, but this injury seriously worried me.

Passing through a little village called Broughton, I stopped in a shop and searched for a curry flavoured Pot Noodle as something to look forward to later that night. Apparently, Storm Francis was going to hit at some point, and I'd had a few worried messages from my mum and a couple of warnings from people on social media. Gavin and Kathi were playing it down, stating that it was 'just a bit of weather'. But it was something else that I couldn't help but bother me.

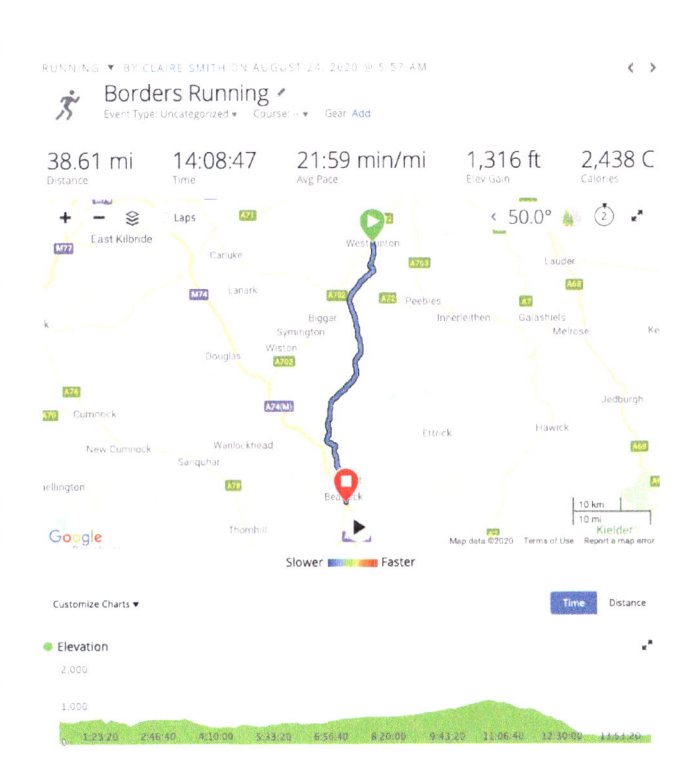

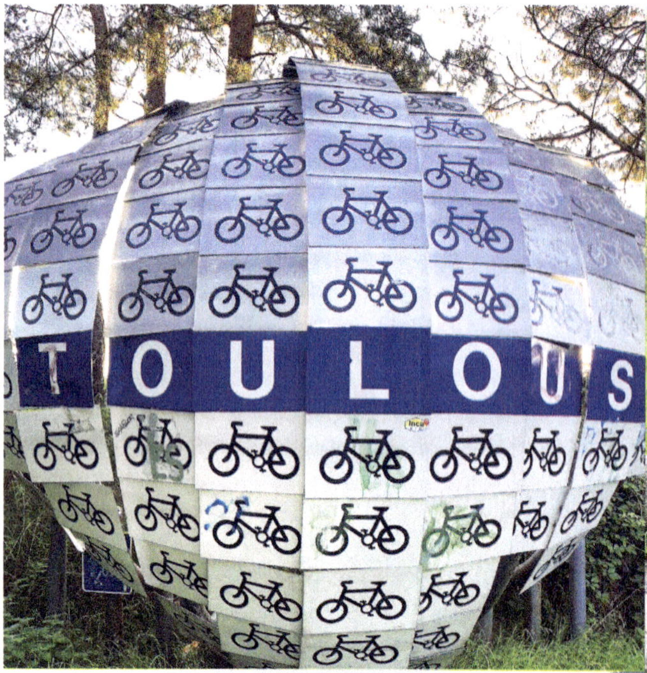
TOULOUS
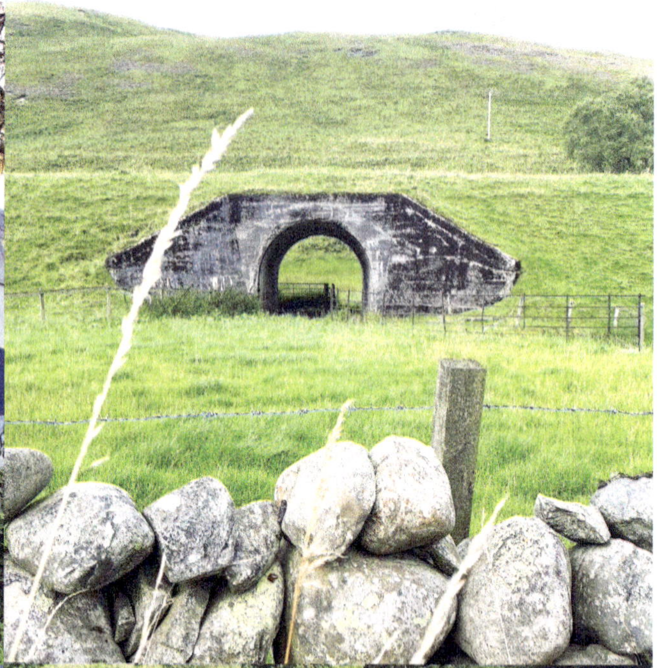
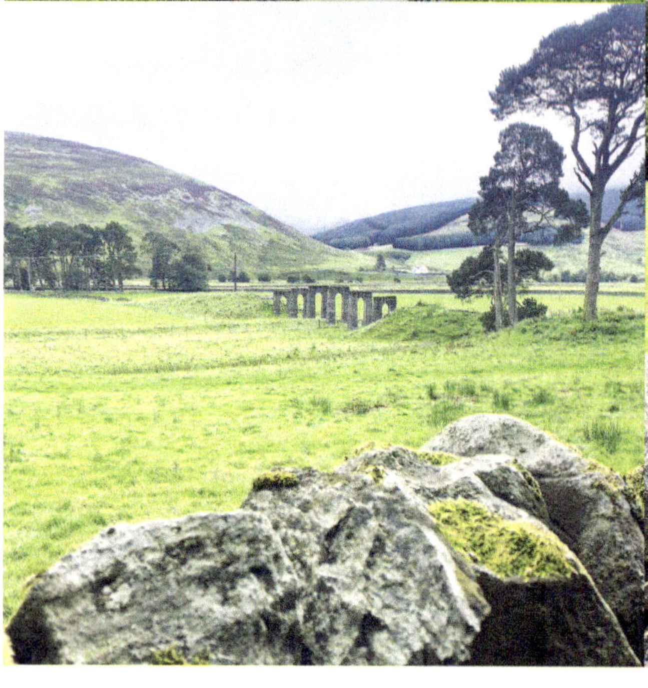
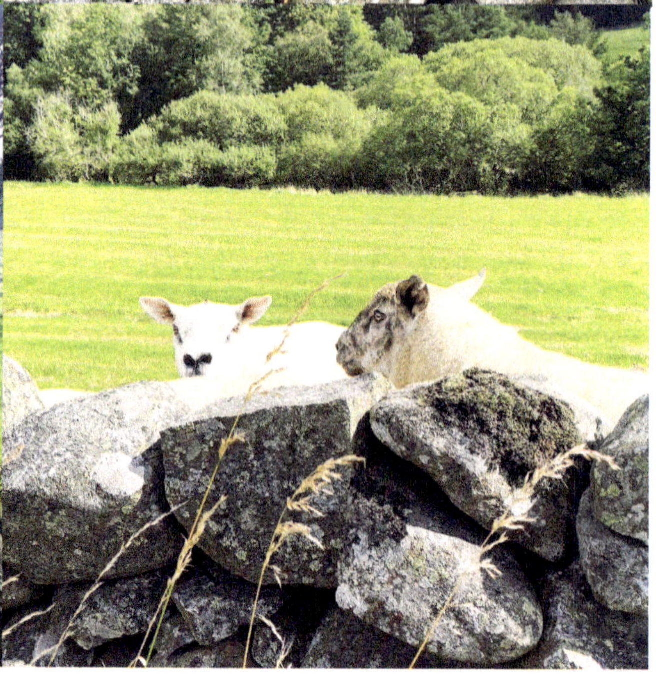

Once I found food for my evening meal and had chosen a few other bits for the rest of the day, I went over to pay. The shop owner asked what I was doing and after I told her, she refused to let me pay for my food. Touched by her kindness, I left feeling a little happier.

The rain stopped and it actually became quite hot for the second time on my JOGLE so far. I peeled off my layers and wondered if I would need to dig about for my sunscreen. Just before mile 19, I found a gateway and stopped to eat a chicken and bacon pie the shop owner had given me. It was delicious. I closed my eyes and let the sun warm my face. While I was lying there, I pulled up my running tights and felt my Achilles. There was a definite lump at the site of the pain, and I was becoming more and more stressed over it. This could actually stop me, I thought. Despite my feelings when I had first woken up this morning, I didn't want to stop. I really wanted to get to Land's End. I massaged the area, swallowed some painkillers and tried to think positively.

The rest of the afternoon consisted of amazing views and wide roads. Huge lorries steaming past me every few minutes, loaded with logs, ruined it a little, but I was becoming hardened to living on the road now. My thoughts kept drifting to my little house, my kids, and my cats. I wanted to be back there today, I was missing home comforts and try as I might to be happy and upbeat, I was struggling. Scotland had been amazing, living up to its reputation in every way. But I was done with it now. I wanted to be back in England. But between me and the border was about 35 miles of road and an impending storm.

That night I found a lovely flat field to camp in. It was next to a church with a large graveyard and a busy A road roared alongside. I set up camp and made my Pot Noodle with the tent door open, as the weather was still good. A little too calm maybe… I wondered if I would be waking up to heavy rain tomorrow. Putting away a soaking wet tent was not fun and would mean everything would be wet for the next night. Whilst I enjoyed my food, I received a message from my lovely friend Koen in the Netherlands. Koen texted me every night with words of support and often a comment on my chosen sleeping spot. As the GPS tracker was so accurate, he could see exactly where I had pitched my tent. I mentioned my concerns about my Achilles, and he sent over a link showing how to strap it with Physio tape. I thanked him and got my first aid kit out ready for the next day, hoping the tape would help.

As I settled down to sleep, I thought back on the day's events. I was not super proud of allowing myself to give into self-pity. The combination of an injury, predicted storm and missing home, was a lot to deal with. But the Achilles was the real issue as it threatened the whole challenge, and that's what was making me negative. As I lay in my sleeping bag, I realised exactly how much I wanted this. The thought of having to stop and get on a train to return home made me feel sick. I remembered how another injury during a Double Deca Triathlon (20 Iron distance triathlons in one go) in Mexico last year almost stopped me, but I had managed to keep moving forward through days of intense pain. Then one morning it began to ease up, and even though the pain never left me, I was able to finish the race. This thought gave me comfort as I drifted off to the sound of lorries on the busy road nearby.

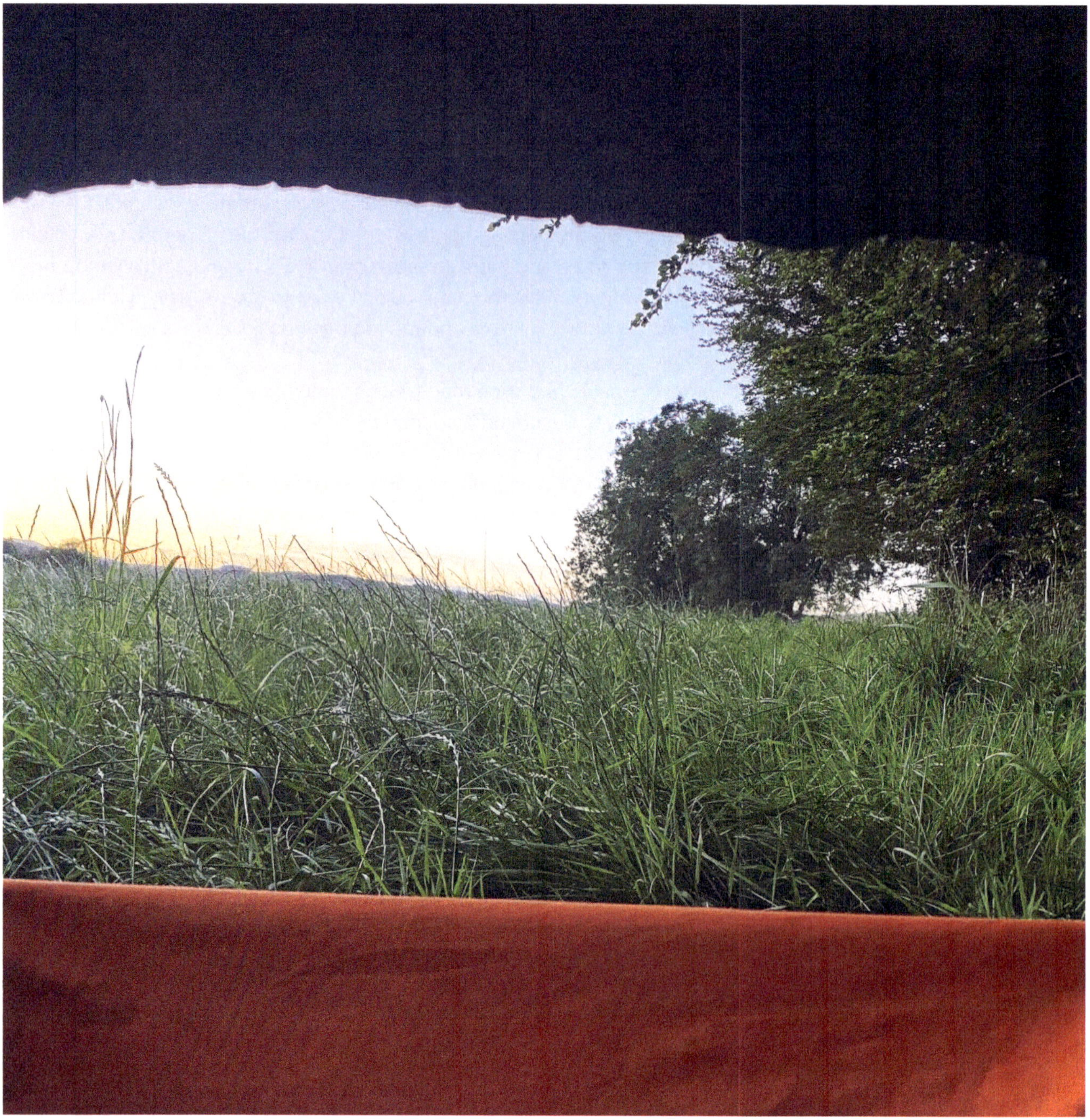

Day 10: Tuesday 25th August
Beattock to Gretna (Storm Francis) - 27.95 miles - Total mileage: 374.77

The alarm on my phone woke me up. I lay there for a moment, listening. No wind or rain. So much for the massive storm, I thought. However, after checking my weather app, it did look like something was on the way. But for now at least, I was grateful for a dry pack down.

Within an hour of being on the road, the rain started. Initially light drizzle, but eventually giving way to strong winds and a torrential downpour. I had already put my waterproofs on, so I was prepared for it. "Screw you, Storm Francis!" I shouted defiantly. "Do your worst". In hindsight, this was a little foolish as three hours later I was not feeling quite so warrior-like, trudging along the side of a very busy road, absolutely soaked. This was going to be a long, long day.

At just over seven miles in, I passed the famous Lockerbie Truckstop. This had been mentioned a fair few times in a JOGLE Facebook group chat I was part of, for being an extremely good place to stop for a fry-up. I hadn't planned on it, but at that moment it suddenly seemed like the best idea ever.

Dodging the lorries pulling into the parking area, I made my way to the entrance. I was a sorry sight, dripping wet and totally bedraggled. I sighed and fixed my soggy face mask around my ears. COVID-19 regulations were in full force, and I had to weave the buggy around one-way systems and through correct doors, trying to understand the signs about what I could and couldn't do. I swore, grateful for the facemask for once.

Once I had placed my order, I sat at a table in the furthest corner. I didn't want a conversation, and all eyes had been on me as I made my way across the room. Bored lorry drivers would have many questions, and on any normal day that would have been fine. But not today.

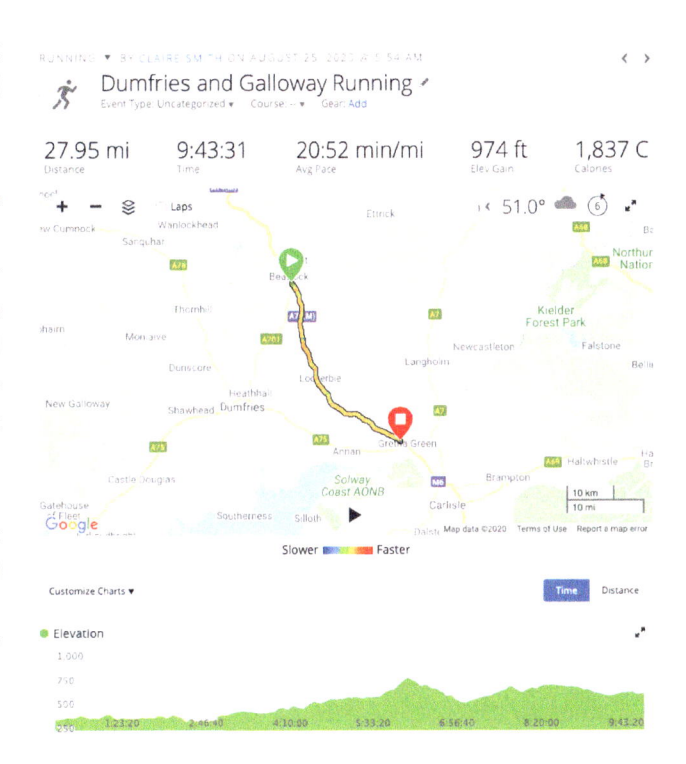

My coffee, tea and food turned up and I literally didn't know what to eat first. I downed the hot coffee, burning my mouth but not caring. I then started shovelling in the egg and chips as quickly as possible. I was shivering cold and didn't want to be stopped for too long. Sometimes I hated not being able to relax, not even for a moment. Only when the day was done and I was far away from my starting point, tucked up in my sleeping bag, could I allow myself to do that. Until then, I was on the clock.

I took a swig of tea and thought about the prospect of camping later. Looking at the weather, it was due to get worse before it got better. A little voice in my head suggested looking at hotels…could I? I checked my planned route for the day and saw that I would go past a motorway service station at Gretna Green that had a hotel. This was great on one hand, but also meant I would still be just shy of crossing the English border which I so desperately wanted to do.

The hotel won. I booked online as I tried, and failed, to finish my food. Why can't I eat more, I wondered. I really needed the calories but got full up so quickly these days. I used the toilets, which was a rare luxury for me, then braced myself for the 21 miles I had to cover to get to a warm hotel. Once back outside, I told myself to focus on the end of the day and stay positive. With the weather and the busy roads, I couldn't even listen to my music or audiobooks today. All I had was eight hours of my own thoughts and that wasn't a particularly inviting prospect.

There was one thing that I was happy about though, and it was a big thing. Before leaving my tent this morning, I had taped my Achilles as Koen had suggested last night, and other than a few twinges early on, I was pain free. I wasn't running at all this day. I had already decided that I needed the recovery, but also running against a strong headwind was a fool's game and would just waste energy. Could it be that the tape was actually working? Whatever it was, I was thankful and hoped that it stayed that way.

At around mile 15 I was so wet that I was becoming really cold. I had already lost a bit of weight and was mindful of becoming mildly hypothermic. I have a lot of experience with the cold, so I knew that I needed to get on top of this before it got to a stage that was harder to come back from. I pulled off the road into a farm. There was a barn I could shelter in and get my down jacket out of the dry bag without getting everything soaked in the process. As I was doing this, a farmer walked past me. I asked if he minded me sheltering for five minutes and he looked confused (pushchair but no baby?), then shook his head. "It's a bad day to be outside" he laughed.

With a warm down jacket under my waterproof and feeling much better, I cracked on. I had another 13 miles to go which seemed like forever, but there was nothing to do but suck it up. Hours later, I finally made it to the services. Checking into my room, I stripped off my waterproofs and wet kit and got straight into a hot shower. It felt amazing. Suitably warmed up, I emptied my dry bag on to the floor and surveyed the contents. There was not a lot of options, but I pulled an outfit together and put on my flip-flops. I needed hot food and supplies for the next day. Walking across the car park without the buggy felt very weird at first, but it was so good to be able to open doors without having to wrestle a huge pushchair through them. It was also nice to just feel invisible for a while. No Hi-Viz and no jogger meant nobody looked my way, wondering what on earth I was up to.

After picking up breakfast and lunch for the following day, I looked around at my options for dinner. Burger King had the smallest queue, so Burger King it was. Once back in my room, I pulled out my cheeseburger, chips and onion rings from the brown paper bag. I was absolutely starving, the cold increasing my normally small appetite. I ate the burger like a wild animal, thankful that nobody was here to witness me stuffing food into my face, sauce going everywhere. As I ate, I half watched A Place in the Sun, whilst catching up with family and friends on my phone.

I was a little bothered that I had only made 28 miles today, but all things considered, maybe it was a blessing in disguise. After I had eaten, I spread my tent and wet kit all over the room. I plugged every device I had into the sockets and finally sat back on my bed. The room looked like a bomb had gone off, but everything was either drying or charging and now I could get under the huge duvet and sleep.

Tomorrow morning, I would cross the Scottish border after 10 long, hard days, to arrive in England.

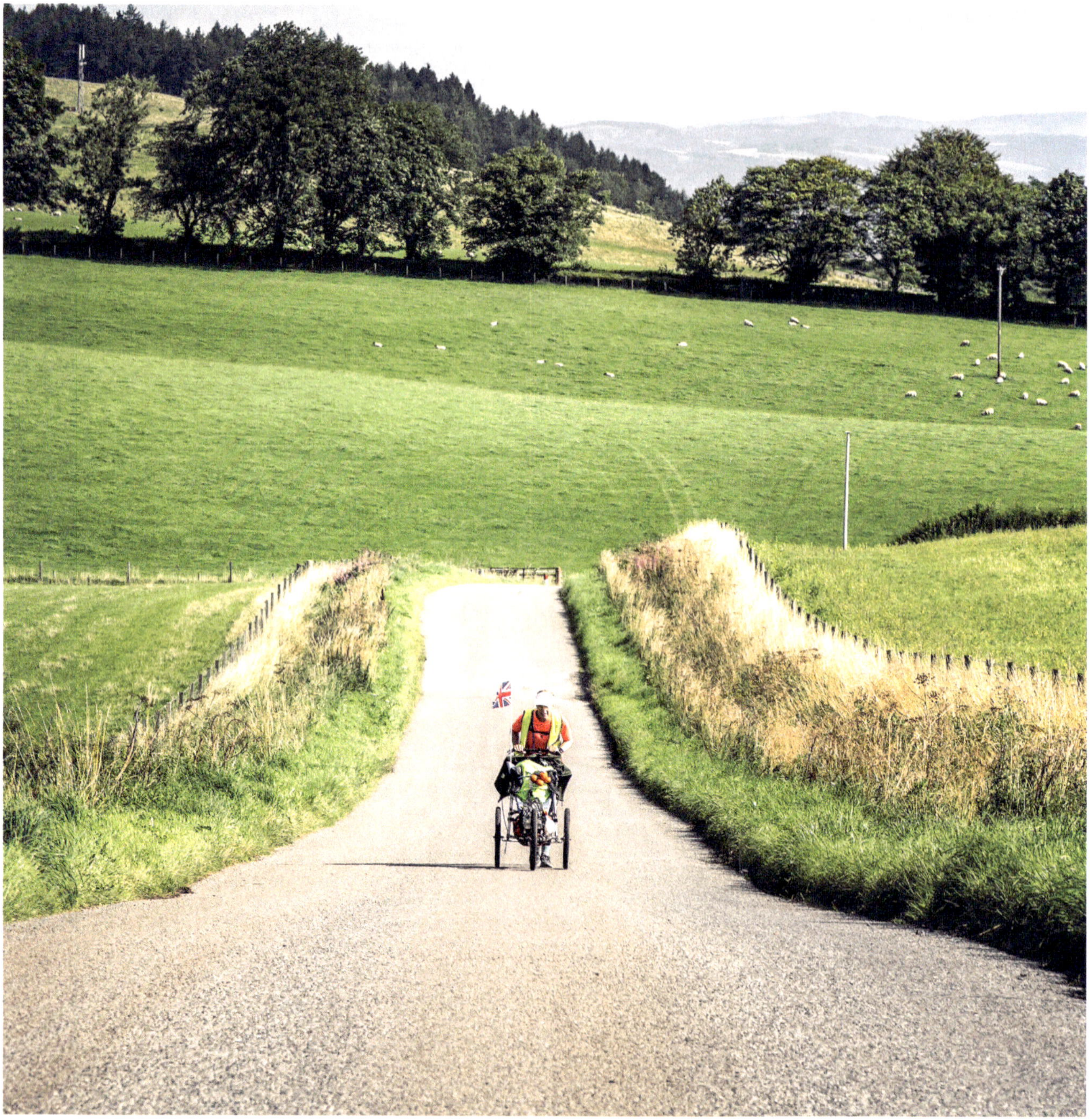

Day 11: Wednesday 26th August
Gretna to Little Strickland - 39.09 miles - Total mileage: 413.86

I had a restless night's sleep, the pain in my feet waking me many times. Why did I always forget how bad they became over ultra-long-distance events? That morning as I hobbled around the hotel room, filling the kettle to make coffee, I decided to put Compeed on the balls of my feet to try and add some padding. It wasn't just blisters that were causing me pain, there was also bruising and nerve damage from repeated impact with the road to contend with.

After just over two miles that morning I finally reached the Scottish boarder. There was a modest sign welcoming me to England and I took a few photos to commemorate and put on social media. I had loved Scotland for its beautiful brutalness, but I was done with it and keen to push on down the country.

The morning went by quickly and I was feeling positive and happy. I was making progress and I felt as if I might actually be able to do this. That was until I got my first puncture. A branch was stuck to my rear tyre, and as I pulled it off, I heard the hiss of air escaping from the tube. This was definitely not going to be a slow one. Within seconds the tyre was completely flat, so I stopped to get the pump and repair kit out of the bottom of my dry bag. I had managed to cross an entire country without getting a single puncture and within hours of being in England I had my first.

I flipped the buggy onto its side and tried to undo the dust cap. I couldn't do it. I tried again, and again, and again. But no matter what I did, I just couldn't do it. Cursing, I looked around and decided to knock on some doors to ask someone to help me. There were only two houses nearby, and nobody answered. I was starting to get a little anxious. I looked back the way I had come, remembering that I had passed a roundabout with a large petrol station on it. I would have to go back,

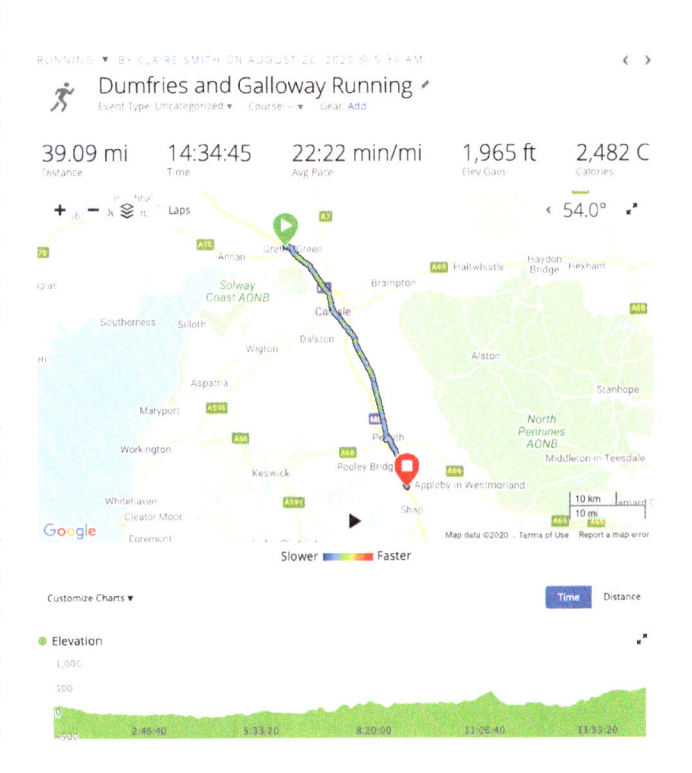

Welcome to
England
Cumbria
Cumbria
County Council

Welcome to
England
Cumbria
dhb

despite hearing endurance legend Wayne Kurtz's voice in my head saying, "Never go backwards!" But I had no choice.

Once at the petrol station, I tried to get someone to help but everyone seemed so busy. Eventually, a man in a suit reluctantly helped and after struggling for a while (which made me feel better) he managed to undo the stubborn dust cap. I thanked him and he disappeared back into his car and drove away. Once I had removed the tyre, I found a new inner tube in my bag and started to try and fit it. It was then that my lack of prep before I left home really bit me on the ass.

The pump I had brought with me did not fit the inner tube.

I wasn't particularly surprised; this is exactly the sort of thing I did on a regular basis. I looked over at the large air pumps for car tyres and realised that they would fit. But after dropping coin after coin in the machine, pressing loads of buttons and having no luck, I started to get really stressed out. I knew this was the worst thing to do, but I just felt so irrational and emotional.

I sat with my head in my hands - what was I going to do? I tried the forecourt shop to see if they sold foot pumps, but they didn't. Despite asking a few people, nobody could or wanted to help me. I was starting to think I would need to find a bike shop, so began searching on my phone. The thought of going even further back on myself was soul destroying. Every mile was so hard to gain, going five or six miles back would be awful.

Suddenly, a man appeared holding a Halfords bag and grinning from ear to ear. "I'm here to save the day!" he announced, and I looked at him in surprise. He pulled out a bike pump and asked, "Will this help?" I breathed a huge sigh of relief and confirmed that yes, it would help massively. John was a lorry driver and on his way to Switzerland. He had his bike with him, planning on doing some riding once he was there, but he'd forgotten his pump from home and had to buy one on the way. Together we fixed the puncture, chatting about what I was doing and laughing about how I had managed to pack the wrong pump.

When we had finished and the buggy was back in the upright position and ready to go again, I gave John a huge hug, not remembering or caring about COVID social distancing rules. I was so thankful to him for giving up his time and helping me. He had saved me hours of trying to find a bike shop and I was so grateful. Once he left, I checked Google and noted there was a Halford's in Penrith where I could buy a new pump and some more inner tubes. Walking away from the petrol station, I gave myself such a serious talking to. "Why the hell did you not check this when you were at home?" I asked myself out loud. "You really are a massive dickhead sometimes".

The rest of the day passed uneventfully. Just before I got to Penrith, whilst walking on a quiet country lane, I came across a tiny field mouse sleeping in the middle of the road. I crouched down and told him that he shouldn't sleep there as he would get squashed. He didn't seem to care and continued sleeping. The road actually looked pretty good in the warm sun of the afternoon and I partly wanted to curl up next to him. But I reminded myself that that's not the sort of thing a sane person does, so I scooped him up and placed him on the side of the road. He looked a little pissed off at me, but then shuffled away into the grass.

The pain in my feet got worse as I descended a huge hill leading into Penrith, wincing with every step. I swallowed some more pain killers and checked where Halfords was on the map. On the way, a man holding a plastic bag walked past me and the smell of fish and chips filled the air. In that moment all I wanted was chips. And curry sauce. Pulling on my face mask, I struggled into the narrow chip shop and within five minutes I was sat on a bench outside, feet up, shoes off, stuffing my face. I sighed, happily. I bloody love chips!

After I had pushed through the rush hour traffic and weaved along busy pavements to buy my bike supplies, I gratefully escaped Penrith. I had covered around 32 miles, and as always, was chasing the Holy Grail of 40. The next few hours took me along some quiet roads with lovely views. The sunset was stunning, so I took a picture for Gavin and Kathi. My pain levels were at an all-time high, but I had discovered that singing (badly) helped in a weird sort of way. The only problem (other than the fact that I can't sing) was I only had one old Madonna song stuck in my head. So, I sang the chorus, over and over again like a crazy person: "When you call my name, it's like a little prayer…"

At mile 37 I began the task of looking for a suitable place to pitch my little tent. It was more challenging than usual on this night, but eventually I found a rough area of ground that seemed unloved. Some rubbish had been dumped in the corner and it was very overgrown. But, over to one side, there was a small patch of flat grass and that was all I needed. Unfortunately, it was still light; I hated setting up camp whilst people could see me. I looked around and saw that there was a big field with about 10 sheep in it, and beyond that, a large farmhouse. Hopefully they weren't looking out of their window at that exact moment.

When I started putting up my tent, I drew the attention of some sheep who made their way over to the corner of the field. They began to push up against the fence, trying to see what I was doing and "Baaaaaing" their questions loudly at me. "Shush!" I said to them, "you're gonna get me caught," but no amount of persuasion would stop them. Eventually I escaped into my tent and hoped they would get bored and leave me alone. I boiled some water, made a Firepot meal of Spaghetti Bolognese and lay back against my pack to eat.

Another tough day, but I had made it to England and amazingly, almost to the halfway point. I settled down with the sound of sheep and the A6 lulling me to sleep.

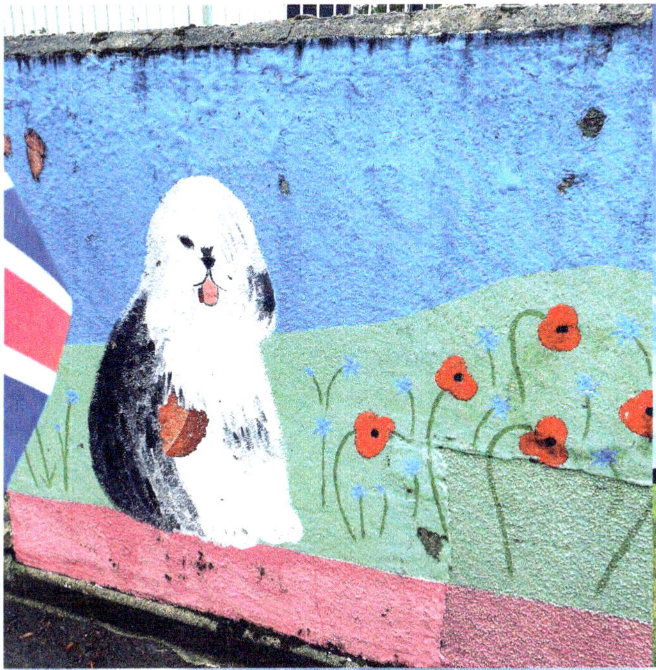
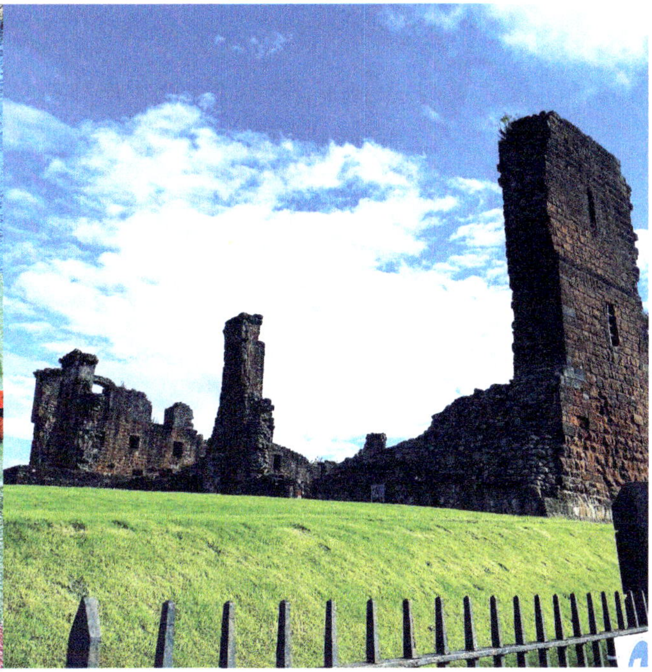
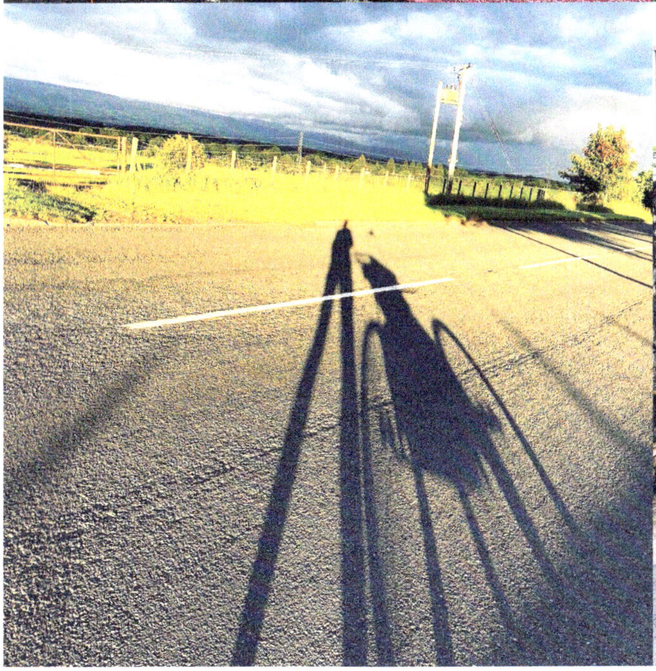
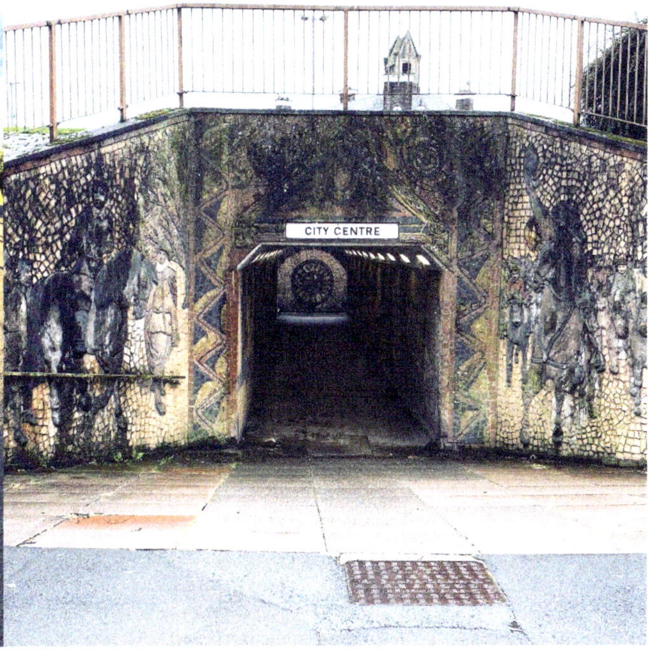
CITY CENTRE

Day 12: Thursday 27th August
Little Strickland to Natland - 23.06 miles - Total mileage: 436.86

I woke up this morning feeling exhausted, but I was keen to push on through the Lakes and get to some flatter areas. That was my motivation, I decided. "Today will be a good day," I said to the sheep who were watching me, thankfully quieter this time. But I felt like I was just saying the words and not really feeling them. My feet were still throbbing from the day before, and I felt completely drained.

I was heading for Shap, which I had been told had a 'bit of a climb'. After going through the little village, a sign warned me that I would soon to be headed for Shap Summit, '1400 feet high and dangerous in winter'. "Brilliant" I muttered. I had no issues with going up, in fact I quite enjoyed the challenge, but going down steep hills with the buggy was just awful. If I had done some training with it before I had left home, I would have known that. But it's not like it would have changed anything, and sometimes not knowing is better.

All morning I struggled to hold it together, but eventually I just let myself cry. I cried over never seeing Susan's smiling face at her door again. I cried over the loss of my relationship that ended a few months previously and how much I missed him. And I cried about the pain in my feet, and how I felt like I was never going to get home.

I pushed the jogger up the steep road through the mist. The air was getting colder. Luckily for much of the climb there was an overtaking lane on one side, so I was able to escape death for another day. Once at the top, I stopped and sheltered in an old phone box. I ate some chocolate and had a good moan to Kathi about anything and everything. "Pull yourself together, Smith" I told myself. But it just wasn't happening today.

The descent was as bad as I expected and by the time I reached the bottom I was broken. The pain in my knees and feet from trying to control the jogger down such a

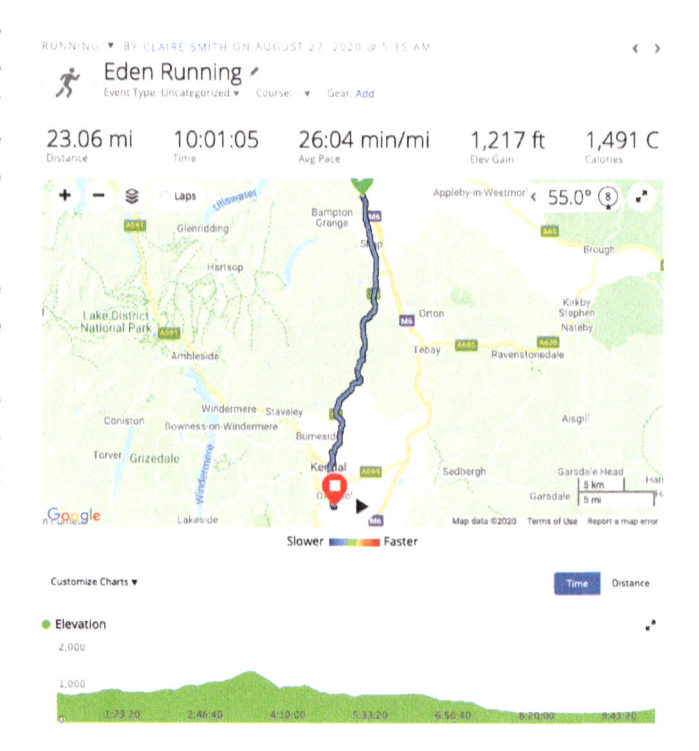

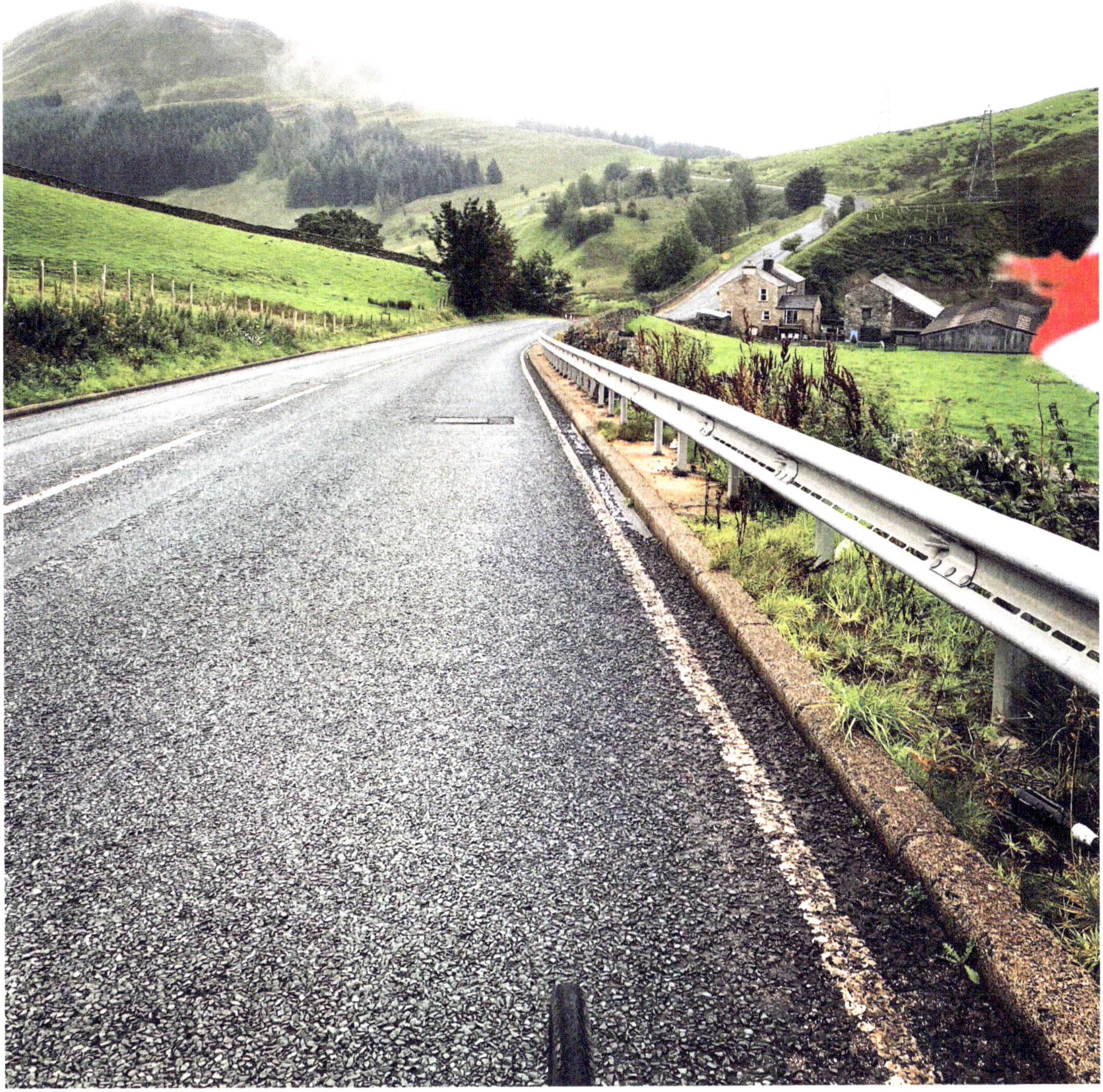

long climb was almost unbearable. The amount of traffic had now increased as well, and I was definitely in the way. I later found out that I'd arrived on a Bank Holiday weekend, which made the roads in the Lake District the worst place to be.

I stopped at a large entrance to what looked like a farm. The sun came out and even though I was still chilly, it felt good on my face. I decided to make a coffee and Pot Noodle in an attempt to rescue the day. If I got in some decent calories and caffeine, things might get better. And that was true for a little while. I had a 10-minute chat with a cyclist which cheered me up, then I pushed on to Kendal.

After another hour or so of fighting traffic and wondering why people become such impatient and inconsiderate idiots when they get behind a steering wheel, I arrived. I headed straight for a supermarket, thinking that a café break and more hot food might help, but due to COVID-19 restrictions it was closed. Taking a deep breath, I said "it's fine" to myself, even though it most definitely was not. I turned around and headed into the superstore feeling very wobbly, you might even say to the point of being unhinged.

So, it was unfortunate when an old woman walked up to me with a purposeful look on her face and said, "I have to tell you this." My heart sank. Whatever she was going to say was probably going to make me burst into tears all over again, and I was desperately trying to hold it together while in such a public place. "We saw you earlier, and *you were on the wrong side of the road!*" She almost shouted at me, waving her hands about. I was a little confused for a moment, as I wasn't expecting her to say that. I sighed and told her that I tried my best to keep out of people's way, but when the road was very winding (as it had been this morning), it was difficult and dangerous to keep changing sides. She didn't seem very happy with this explanation, but I had to quickly turn and walk away, because what I really wanted to say was "Did you *really* have to come up and say that to me? Did it not occur to you that I didn't really want to be in the road either?" I thought the fact that I had the words "John o' Groats", "Land's End" and "Unsupported" plastered across my back might give people a little clue as to what I was doing. Apparently not.

I walked away feeling angry and incredibly lonely at that moment. I grabbed some water, sandwiches and more Compeed and got out of there before anyone else could speak to me. I needed to get away from the Lake District, and people in general, as fast as possible.

Walking as quickly as I could, I got through Kendal and kept going. I wanted to find somewhere to take a break. I needed to stop fighting the day, accept that it wasn't going to improve, and that the best option was to rest. I went past a farmer's field and looked in. The path seemed to lead up to what looked like some kind of service building, with a railway line behind it. I looked around me and decided to risk it. Undoing the gate quickly, I pushed

SHAP FELL BOTHY

A 6 to Kendal
via Shap Summit
Altitude 1400 feet
Winter Conditions
can be dangerous

the jogger up the path before anyone could see me. Once at the top of the field, I saw the building was something to do with the water company. This was good news. There was also an area where I could pitch my tent that was out of sight from people. This was important because it was still the middle of the afternoon and hours from getting dark.

After I had put up my tent, I set about boiling water and sorting my kit. I worked out that if I got up very early tomorrow, I could have 12 hours rest here. This is exactly what I needed, some decent recovery and time off my feet. My mum was messaging me, trying to work out what I was up to, so while I waited for my food to cook, I called her. Once again, the floodgates opened and I sobbed while I told her everything that had happened and how bad I felt. It must have been so hard for her, listening to me and not being able to do anything. After we had said goodbye, she messaged to ask if I wanted her and Alan to drive up from Bournemouth. I replied that I would be fine tomorrow and not to worry.

Before I went to sleep, I looked at where I was headed the next day. The large city of Preston was a little over 40 miles from me. I also saw there was a Premier Inn at that point. I had only managed 23 miles today and I needed to make sure that tomorrow I hit 40. I booked the hotel as a way to ensure I did exactly that, then settled down to dream of hot baths and large, comfy hotel beds the next day.

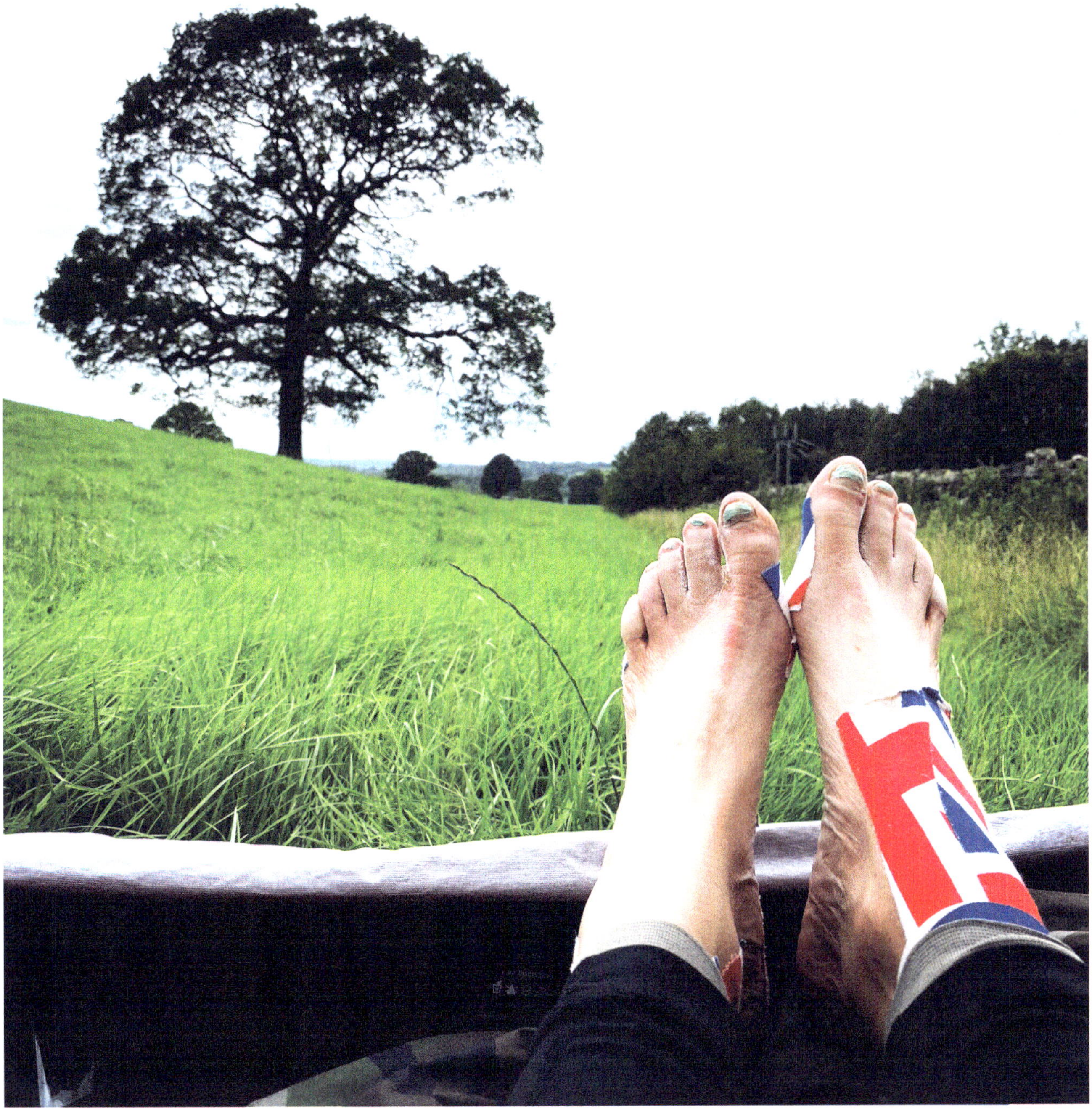

Day 13: Friday 28th August
Natland to Preston - 43.32 miles - Total mileage: 480.18

After my mega-break of 12 hours I felt good, back in a positive state of mind. Before I got out of my tent, I drained my blisters, cleaned and dried my feet, and applied a 'Compeed Sandwich'. This consisted of a large Compeed plaster applied to the balls of my feet, then a large strip of physio tape, and finally another Compeed on top of that. I wasn't sure how much difference it would make, but I was desperate for some relief from the pain in my feet.

It was raining, obviously, as I was still in the Lake District. By the time I'd walked across the thick grass from where I'd set up camp to the road, my trainers were wet through. Not good, as I really needed to keep my poor feet as dry as possible if the blisters were to stand a chance of healing. Once I was through the farmer's gate and had retied the string that was holding it closed, I walked straight into an enormous puddle that I hadn't seen in the darkness. One foot was now completely soaked. Yesterday this would have broken me, but today I just shrugged and started to run.

I trotted down dark country lanes with my audiobook keeping me company, happy that I felt so much better and looking forward to my hotel room later that day. I needed to keep my pace up to ensure I arrived early enough to make the most of it. Turning a corner, I came to a railway tunnel that was marked with flood warning signs. There was a water level pole further in. I could also see the tunnel was already completely full of water. I stopped. I literally didn't know what to do. It was still dark so I couldn't make out how long the tunnel was, or how deep the water.

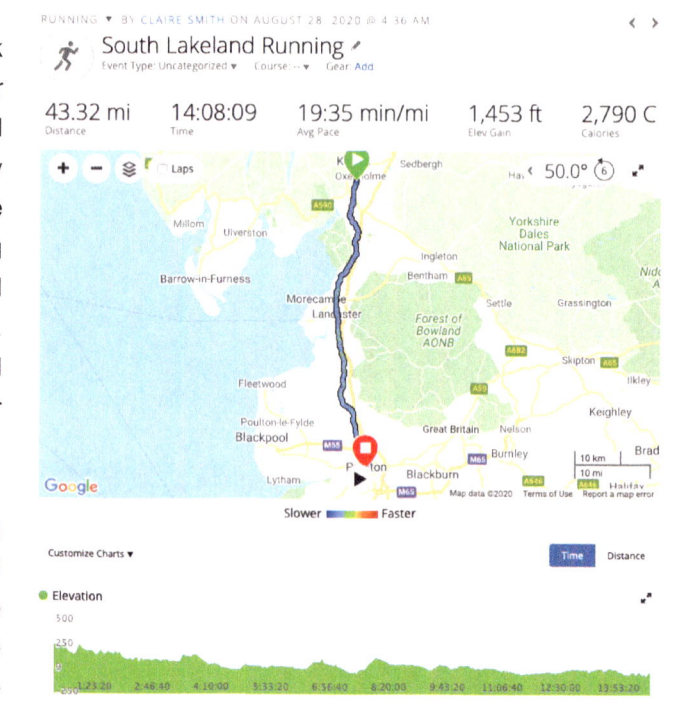

There was something that felt wrong about just walking into this tunnel. As I stood there, it became more and more scary. I had visions of the water lapping over the sides of the buggy and rising up my legs. "Don't be so ridiculous," I said out loud, but still I couldn't make myself do it. I was too aware that wading through would loosen all the Compeed and tape that I had painstaking applied that morning, and that my feet, which were already wet, would be absolutely soaked for the rest of the day.

Looking around me, I tried to find another route. But there was nothing, so I had no choice but to go through the tunnel. Taking a deep breath, I pushed the jogger into the cold water and went into the darkness. The flood water came to just over my ankles, but as I went further into the tunnel it stayed at that level. After a little while, I saw the light at the end and relief washed over me. Once I was out and back onto the road, I laughed at how scared I had been and how I had made the situation much worse by panicking and letting my imagination get the better of me.

The rain got heavier as my route turned onto a muddy canal foot path. Whilst crossing a bridge I saw a parked car and as I got closer, a man jumped out wearing a Brutal Duathlon t-shirt. He said hello, and that he had been following my progress since I started. He went on to say that my route would take me past his front door, and would I like a coffee? That was the best news I had heard for a while and I said how lovely that would be. The smiley man (who must have told me his name, but I wasn't retaining much by that point), jumped back in his car and said that he would see me later.

Once I was off the canal path and back on roads, Smiley Man reappeared. He walked with me for a while, chatting about Brutal and his training, whilst the rain continued to fall and drip down my back. As he talked, I noticed that the jogger felt a little off balance and wondered why. After about five minutes I realised I had another puncture. Hardly surprising after all the off-road sections we had been over that morning. Luckily, we were close to Smiley Man's house and he made me the most amazing coffee and pressed a box of 'posh biscuits' into my hands. "Only the best here" he laughed, and I sat in his garage as he set about fixing my puncture for me.

I left that house feeling so happy. I think the caffeine and sugar hit was part of it, but also I felt an overwhelming sense of gratitude for the lovely people that were following my journey and taking time out of their day to support me. The rain finally stopped, and I felt really strong, pushing my pace up and ticking off the miles. More and more people popped up to say hello over the morning and into the afternoon. A lady who called herself 'The Running Granny' (the oldest woman to have ran the JOGLE), pulled over in her camper van and made me tea and scones. While I sat there eating and talking about the challenges of running the length of the UK, a man and his daughters appeared at the door of the camper to offer more words of support and ask if I wanted some home-made curry. I politely declined as I wasn't hungry, but I was also starting to feel a little anxious over the time I was spending talking to people. I still had a long way to go to the centre of Preston.

Back on the road and running again, I passed another group of ladies with cowbells, all shouting and clapping their encouragement. I beamed at them as I ran past. As I left the built-up area, I switched on my music to help keep my pace up. A few miles down the road I saw what I thought was a giant squirrel in the lay-by. "It can't be" I said to myself in disbelief. "It is!" I squealed. It was the Brutal Squirrel! I had met Justin years ago when my business partner, James Page, had completed my Double Iron race. He had been dressed as a giant yellow Minion back then, and his personality was as big as his stature. At well over 6 feet tall, he was larger than life and you could always hear him coming before you actually saw him. From then on, he became a familiar face at my races. Justin would help with whatever job needed doing, and he also took on the role of the Brutal Squirrel to support the athletes. He loved nothing more than to jump out of the bushes as exhausted, hallucinating competitors ran past, scaring the living daylights out of them.

I was so pleased to see him that I burst into tears and gave him a massive hug. He asked me where I was headed, and I told him that I had about 18 miles left to get to the hotel in Preston. Justin asked if he could stay with me, driving ahead and stopping at lay-bys to keep me company. I told him that I would love that, and it would help keep me going.

The afternoon went by quickly with Justin (now back in human form) waving as he drove past me and cheering as I ran. I was within six miles of the hotel when the familiar, throbbing pain in my feet started again, slowing me to a walk. The last few miles were going to be tough, but I appreciated how far I had come that day and knew that I just had to suck it up for a couple of hours. By singing, deep breathing, and taking some more painkillers, I finally made it to the hotel. It was in the centre of Preston, busy with cars and people. Dealing with the frenetic pace of the city on top of the pain in my feet was a real struggle, so I was glad to see the familiar sign of the Premier Inn in front of me. I said goodbye to Justin who promised to come and see me again at some point further down the country, then limped up to my room.

Closing the door behind me, I breathed a big sigh of relief. I stopped my Garmin, which read 43 miles. Christ, I was feeling every one of them right now. I pulled off my trainers and socks and lay on the bed. "Fuuuuuccckkkk!!" I moaned. How was it possible that my feet could hurt this much? I forced myself to get up, dry my wet kit, and put all my devices on charge. I then ran a bath and made myself drink a pint of water. I tried not to think about the damage I was doing to myself with the copious amounts of painkillers I was taking, and never quite managing to drink enough.

Sat in the bath, I tentatively pulled at the soggy tape and Compeed on the bottoms of my feet. I winced in pain as they stuck to the skin and tore it off. Limping out of the bathroom, I crawled on to the bed and massaged my poor feet. I then placed pillows under my legs to elevate them and help reduce the pain. I received a message from my best friend Claire, so I messaged back, explaining the state I was in. She replied with the following:

"Ok. I'm gonna say it and please don't be mad, but if it's that bad - please don't carry on. You are too precious. It's hard to know you are in so much pain. xxx"

That rocked me a little. I couldn't stop, could I? I briefly played out the scenario in my head and then quickly pulled myself back to reality. No, I was doing this for Claire's mum, Susan. Giving up would be awful and I would never forgive myself for it. I would just keep putting one foot in front of the other, and eventually I would get to the end.

I had to.

Day 14: Saturday 29th August
Preston to Stretton - 34.63 miles - Total mileage: 514.81

The next morning was bright and sunny. My feet and legs still hurt like hell, but after a good night's sleep I was mentally in a much better place than just a few hours before. As I left the hotel, I felt ready to face the day. Decent rest had lifted my mood, but I was also looking forward to staying in another Premier Inn tonight. My route was becoming progressively more urban, which made it much harder to find places to camp. The hotel was only 34 miles away, which was an added bonus.

Almost immediately though, I met my first obstacle. The bridge across the River Ribble was shut for repairs which meant I had to find an alternative route. Fortunately, the detour didn't add too much extra mileage, so I kept moving on through the streets with the early morning commuters. I was definitely missing the countryside now that I was heading further south. It made life a little harder, as it wasn't as easy to find places for a sneaky wee break, or even just a field to stop and put my feet up.

During the morning, as I went through busy towns bustling with people doing their Saturday shopping, a man jumped out of his car and ran across the road to meet me. It was Gordon who I had met during DecaUK in Dorney back in 2017, when he took part in the Double Iron triathlon event I was organising. It was so good to see a familiar face. After a hug and a brief chat, he promised to see me later that morning.

The day went by in a blur of towns, cars and people. As promised, Gordon appeared in a few places. Once with one of the biggest bacon butties I had ever seen, and the next with a famous Wigan Pie. What a brilliant guy, I was so touched by the effort he made to help me that day.

At around 14 miles, I was finally treated to a small section of countryside and found a field where I could put my

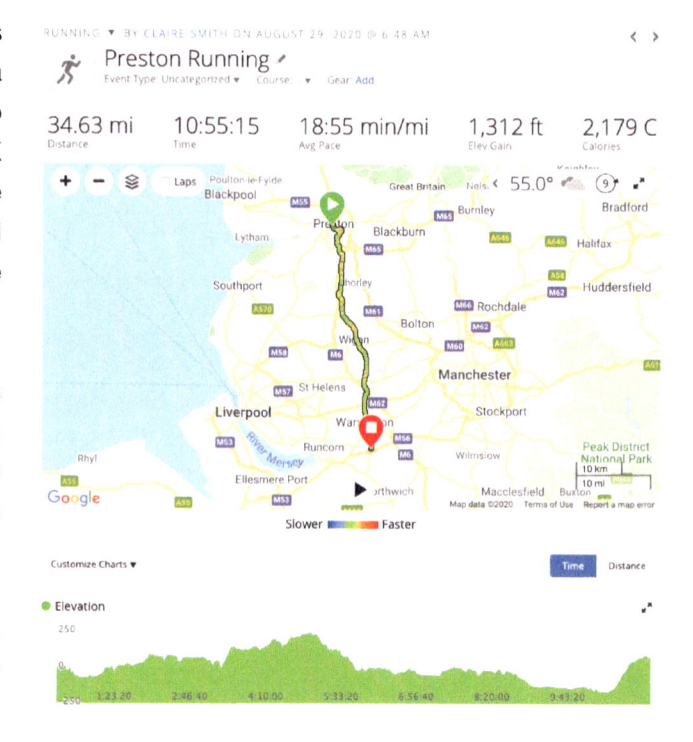

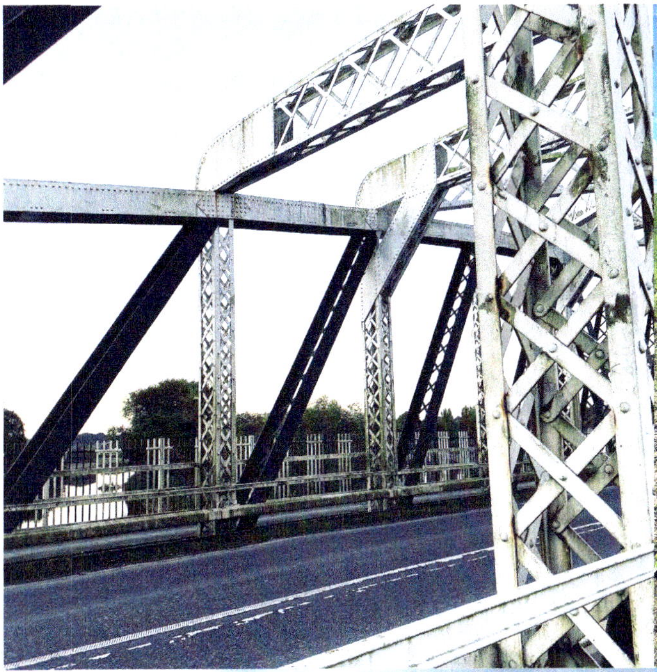

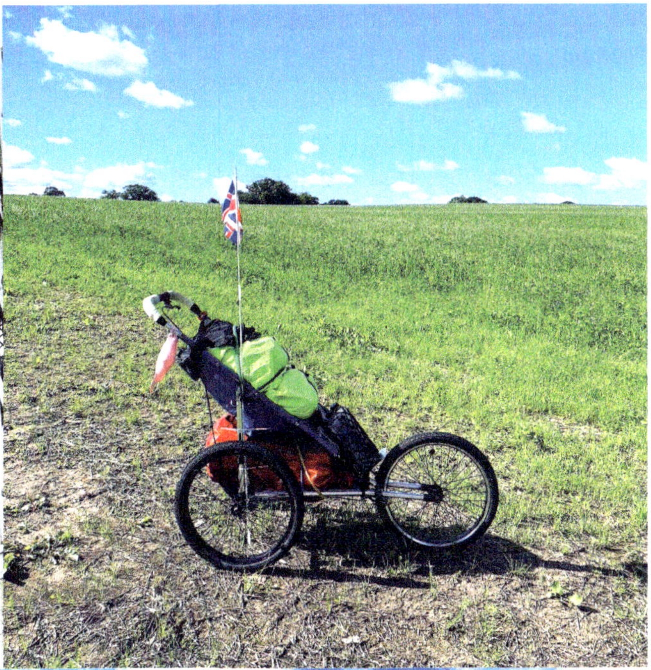

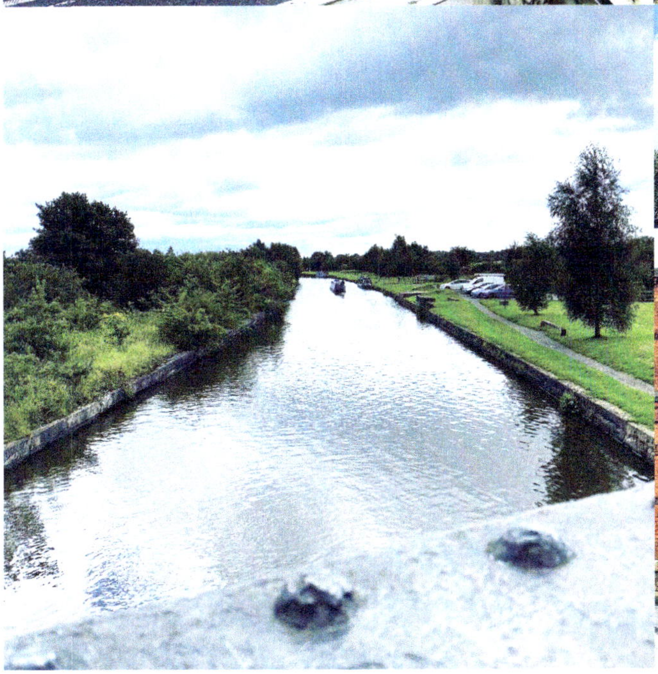

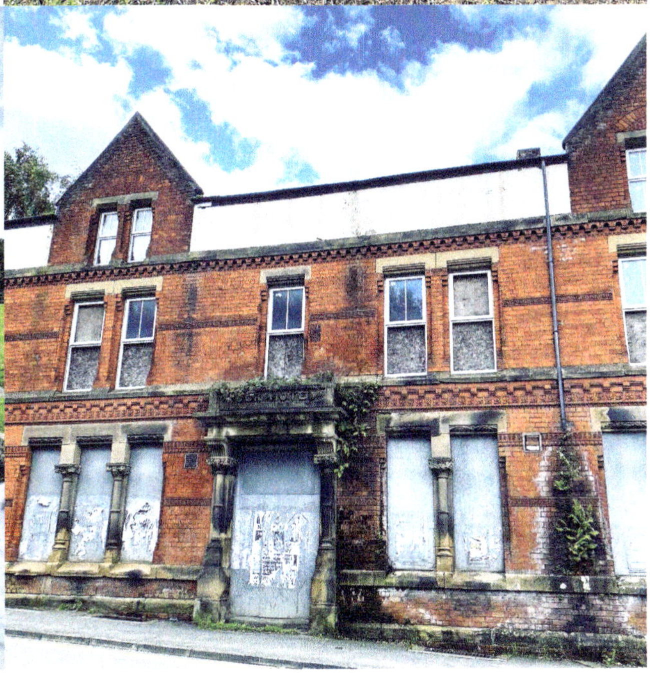

feet up and have a short break. The sun was out, my feet were dry, and I enjoyed feeling relaxed. A drama-free day was exactly what I needed.

Back on the road again, I made my way through Wigan and headed to Warrington. The roads soon turned from quiet lanes to busy dual carriageways. Passing a Starbucks, I decided to treat myself to a latte and got off my feet for 20 minutes. Normally I am a big fan of coffee shops, but recently they had lost their appeal a little. I would struggle through the doors with my huge baby-less pushchair, flag and Hi-Viz, and people would just stare at me. Then they would quickly look down at their drinks, seemingly embarrassed, avoiding all eye contact. It was so strange. When I was on the roads I would get endless support, but here in a coffee shop I seemed to make people uncomfortable. Once I had my order I would drink my coffee, feel every bit the freak, and be keen to escape as quickly as possible.

Warrington was even busier than Wigan. I kept my head down as I passed through the busy town centre. A group of drunk blokes tried to get my attention, pointing and laughing at me. I felt my anger levels rising but forced myself to keep walking and ignore them. "Just focus on getting to the Premier Inn," I told myself.

Rain started to fall as I got closer to Stretton. Just as I pulled my coat on, I looked up to see a large figure walking towards me. Big Dave! He had messaged me before I had started the JOGLE to say that he would see me at some point up North. Dave Kershaw had completed The Double Brutal and both versions of the DecaUK Ultra Triathlon (1x10 and Continuous). He had also finished the Arch to Arc, which has been on my bucket list for many years. It is, in my opinion, the hardest triathlon in the world, because to complete it you have to swim the English Channel! Dave and I had spent many hours chatting about training and preparing for it.

Dave kept me company until I arrived at the hotel, and I was very grateful for the distraction from my screaming feet. Once I got inside, I looked around and noticed they had given me a disabled room. This was perfect as it meant more room for the jogger, and the bath and toilet both had handrails. These were becoming more and more useful for me, because as soon as I clicked the stop button on my Garmin my body seemed to take it as a cue to completely seize up, and I could barely move.

Once the daily routine of kit sorting, charging my phone, watch and tracker was complete, I lay in the bath, closed my eyes and wondered what the next day had in store for me.

KATE'S COTTAGE

JOHN O'GROATS
495 Miles
LAND'S END
318 Miles

Day 15: Sunday 30th August
Stretton to Alderton - 41.67 miles - Total mileage: 556.48

I was up and running at 5:00am. My spirits were high again, and I made good progress along the quiet roads. I was grateful that it was Sunday, and the traffic would be light for a few more hours. Just before nine miles, I could see someone who seemed to be wearing a wetsuit, standing by the side of the road. As I got closer, I could see that it was another ultra-triathlon friend, 'Deca Dave' Clamp. He was famous for completing more deca triathlons than anyone else in the UK. Not only could he go long, he was also fast and had qualified for Kona, and is a former Double Deca World Record Holder. Dave was off to swim at his local lake (hence the wetsuit) but wanted to catch me before he left. I had known Dave for many years, and we had been at a few ultra-races together in Switzerland and Mexico. It was great to see him after so long and we talked about how we were missing the ultra-scene due to the pandemic.

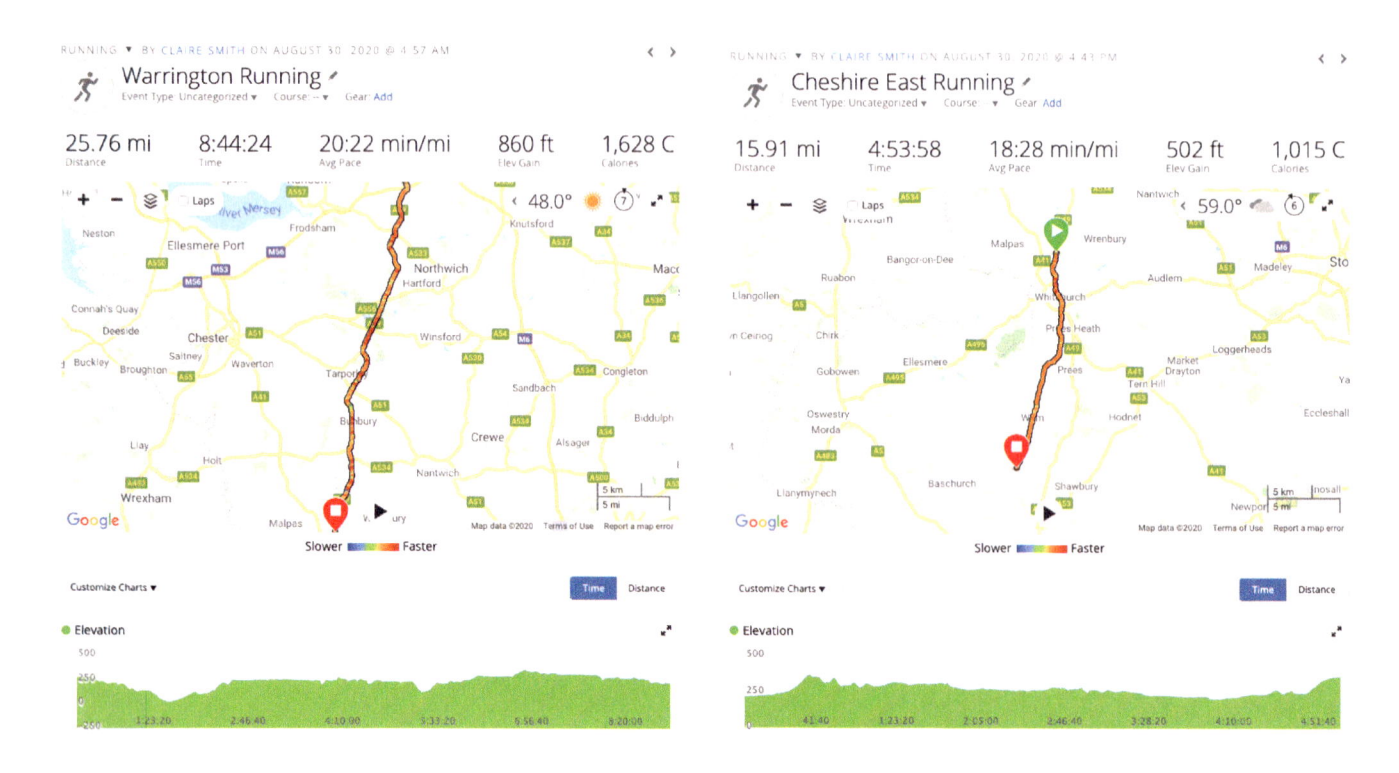

After leaving Dave to his training, I continued down the road and turned a corner to find a large petrol station with a Costa's sign in the window. Coffee was exactly what I needed right now, and I was also running low on food. After stocking up and treating myself to a huge latte and Danish pastry, I was back on the road again.

I could feel it was going to be a warm day as I made my way along the quiet country lanes. I was feeling positive this morning, as when I looked at my tracker on the map (as I did, obsessively), I could see that I was getting closer to Cornwall. It was still a very long way off, but my addled brain was already starting to try and work out how long I had left, and what day I might finish on. It was definitely still too early to say, so I had to be careful not to focus on the finish too much when there were still hundreds of miles to go.

Turning another corner, I saw three people waiting on the side of the road. I immediately recognised one as my head event medic and very good friend, Pouch. I had met Paul (real name, believe it or not) on the first event I had ever organised back in 2012, and we had been great friends ever since. We have been through a lot of tough times together, running events that go on for days or sometimes weeks. Pouch had been a massive support to me over the years and here he was again, this time holding a large bag of white chocolate and raspberry cookies for me.

After chatting and laughing with Pouch and his family for 15 minutes or so, I reluctantly left them and went on my way. The traffic was starting to get a little heavier with many motorbikes and sports cars speeding down the narrow lanes towards me. It was a Bank Holiday weekend, and the sun was out. That was a rarity in the UK, and I had a sinking feeling that my day was going to get harder very soon.

I was right. It wasn't long before I found myself on the A49, battling traffic once again. It felt much worse than usual; although still an A road, it was narrow, and the cars and lorries were driving very fast. I tried to remain positive, but after a few hours of inconsiderate idiot drivers, I pulled off the road into the driveway of a stately home for a break.

I sat with my head in my hands, looking at my phone, trying to see how long I was on this bloody road for. To my dismay, I saw it would be a long time. At that moment, another medic friend, Chris from Brutal turned up with his girlfriend to say hello. Although I was really happy to see them, I found it hard to hide my feelings over my struggles with the busy traffic. There was nothing I could do about it though. With no alternative routes on offer, I simply had to suck it up and get back to it.

After 25 miles, I finally broke and decided to stop and find somewhere to camp for a few hours. Maybe the roads would be quieter by then, or at least I would be in a better place mentally and physically to deal with it. I found an area of scrub in the corner of a farmer's field and decided to risk it. The worst thing that could happen was I would be told to move on. I made myself a Pot Noodle and then settled down to sleep for a while. It was strange being in the tent whilst it was still so warm, but I enjoyed it and drifted quickly off to sleep.

After a few hours, I woke and pulled on my trainers. I packed down the tent and loaded the buggy. A quick tyre check (I now did this about a hundred times a day) told me I had yet another puncture. Pulling out a new inner tube, pump and tyre levers, I flipped the jogger on its side and changed the tube. I had become quite an expert at this now and it only took me a few minutes. Which, compared to the hour it took me to fix my first puncture, was a big improvement.

However, I was really starting to worry about the buggy making it to Land's End. I had begun to joke about who would break first, me or the jogger. Even though I made light of it, it was a real concern. I went up and down hundreds of curbs throughout the day, and although I tried to be careful, the weight of my kit and the unknown age and condition of the buggy made me wonder if one day it would just snap. It was out of my control, so I tried not to waste energy on stressing over it too much. But I won't lie, it was in the back of my mind a lot.

As the day turned into late afternoon and then early evening, the traffic and my mood greatly improved. The JOGLE was one long rollercoaster of emotions, and sometimes getting off the ride for a few hours to rest was the best and only thing I could do. I needed to cover another 15 miles to hit the magic 40 and I knew that I would be able to do that easily. It would mean pushing on later than normal, and I would need my head torch and lights for the buggy, but it was achievable.

By 10:00pm, I was done. It had got very dark and the temperature was dropping rapidly. The darkness made it harder to find somewhere to camp, but eventually I found a flat field with an open gate, so I pushed the buggy off the road. Once I had set up camp, I pulled my down jacket out of my dry sack. I was already cold, and I knew it would get colder as the night went on. My two-season sleeping bag had been enough up to now, but I had a feeling I would be testing its limits tonight.

I made a hot meal and settled down for some much-needed sleep.

Day 16: Monday 31st August
Alderton to Ludlow - 39.9 miles - Total mileage: 596.38

After shivering in my tent for what seemed like most of the night, I gave up. It was 3:00am and I was absolutely freezing. I decided that I might as well be moving so I could at least warm up. I checked the weather app on my phone and it read four degrees. It definitely felt like it.

This morning I was headed for the large town of Shrewsbury. Switching on my head torch again, I made good progress along the quiet roads with Alastair Humphrey's audio book about cycling around the world to keep me company. I couldn't run much because I was literally wearing *all* my clothes, but I was still cold. I had a feeling this wasn't just down to the temperature, but also my noticeable weight loss, extreme tiredness and dehydration.

I made it to Shrewsbury just as the sun was rising. I was desperate for a hot drink and some good food. I had been dreaming of a steamy café serving cooked breakfasts (I was *still* craving fried bread) and big mugs of tea. But it was too early for anything to be open, despite me walking around in circles trying to find something, anything.

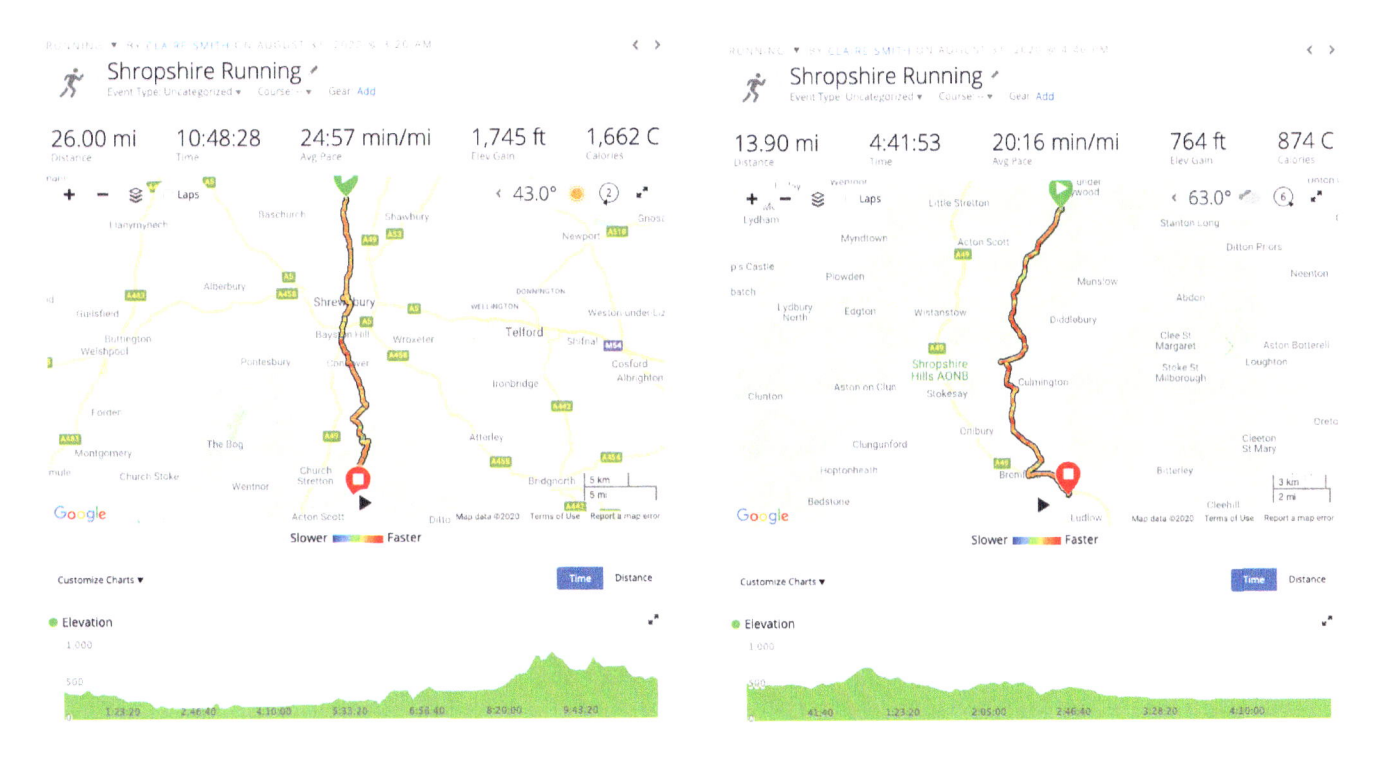

I had very little food left but found some chocolate in my pocket, so bit into a couple of squares. Almost immediately I regretted it, as the cold temperature had made the normally soft Dairy Milk rock hard and a large chunk of my tooth broke off. I flinched with pain. I suddenly felt like my body was starting to fall apart - this was the last thing I needed right now. The remaining tooth was sharp, jagged, and I caught my tongue on it continuously.

I eventually found a garage that was open and went inside to buy water, some food that was easy to eat (and wouldn't cause more damage to my crumbling teeth), and some much-needed coffee. I then found a park bench and sat down to eat my yogurt and drink latte. A few tears rolled down my face and I didn't bother brushing them away. I had a new-found empathy for anyone unfortunate enough to find themselves homeless, because in that moment it was exactly how I felt, incredibly low and very lonely. I allowed myself a good ten minutes to wallow in self-pity whilst I ate, too sad to care about the looks I got from people passing by. I was well aware that I did not look like an athlete in any way. I was tired, unwashed, cold and miserable.

Hauling myself off the bench, I pressed on over a dual carriageway. And then I stopped. "Pack in this feeling sorry for yourself bullshit right now. You chose to be here, remember?" I said to myself, as I had done many times before over the last 16 days. I found a bus stop, which luckily nobody was using, and parked up to sort myself out. Pulling out my hairbrush, toothbrush and medical kit, I set to work.

My feet were a disgusting mess again as I had neglected them last night and this morning. They were oozing some kind of yellow gunk that made me feel sick. I pulled the tape off and gently tugged at the Compeed. After a little persuasion and wincing, both feet were dressing-free. I gave them a good clean and a dusting of medicated talc, then decided to put just one Compeed on each foot. I would see how that felt over the morning before I added any more padding.

Once I had cleaned my teeth and brushed my hair, I felt so much better. The sun was warming me up and the food and caffeine had kicked in too. I refused to let a bad start dictate the rest of the day. Not long after I had left my bus stop spa break, a lady and her two children caught up with me. They introduced themselves and told me how they had been following my progress since they first saw me on Instagram. The young girl told me how her mum 'kept crying over my little dot moving down the screen everyday'. This was so touching, and I was blown away by how my journey was affecting people that I had never even met. They stayed with me for about 20 minutes, chatting about their lives, lifting my mood even more. Just as they were about to leave, the lady pressed a ten-pound note into my hand. "This is for you to get a good coffee and some cake" she said. "I've already donated to the charity, so this is yours". Tears filled my eyes, but this time they were happy ones. I thanked her for her generosity and for cheering me up so much. As they turned and walked back to their car I was struck once again by the JOGLE rollercoaster, how I could go from feeling my lowest one minute to being so high the next.

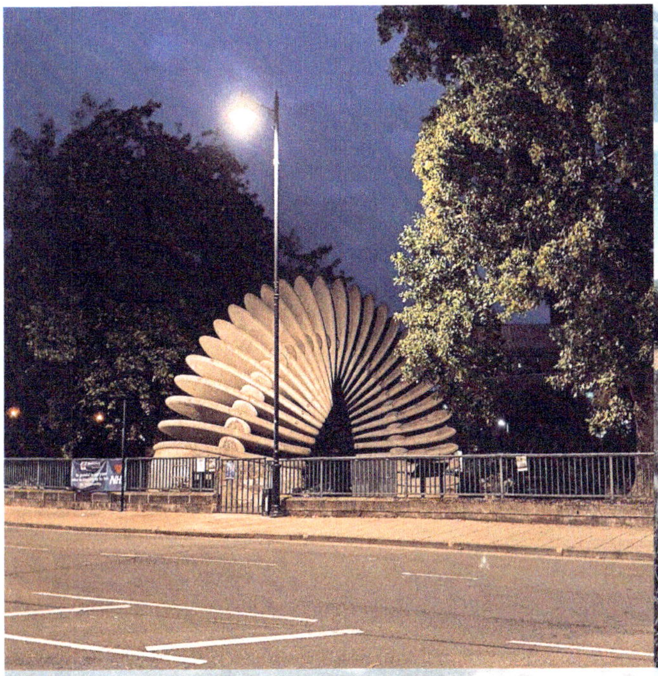
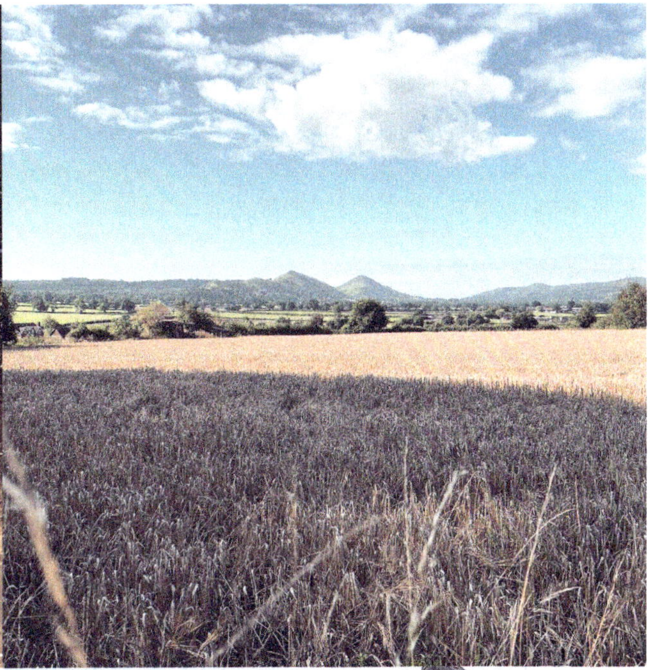
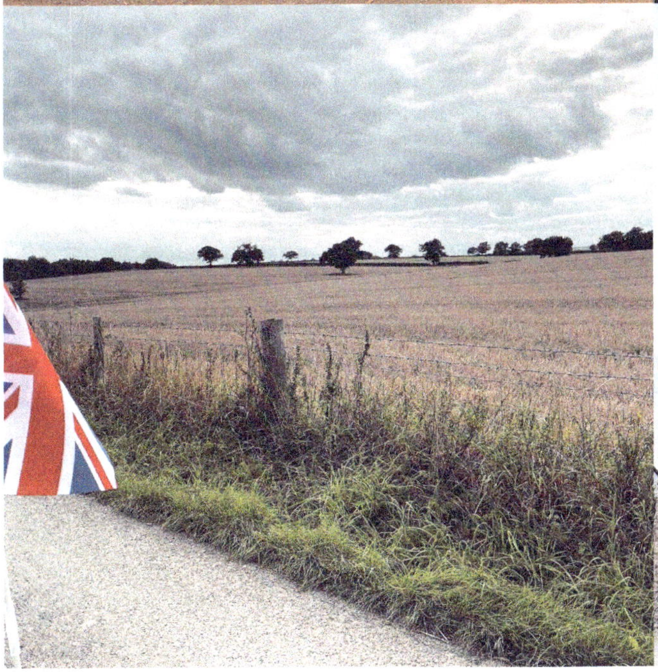
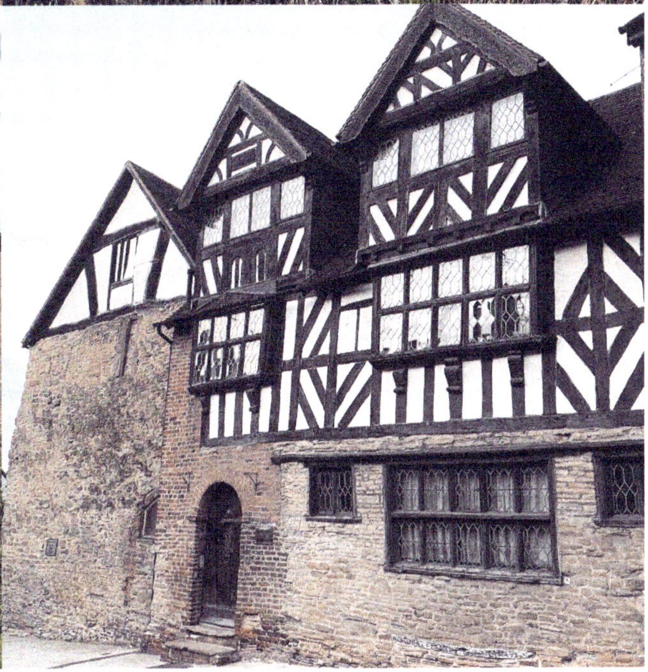

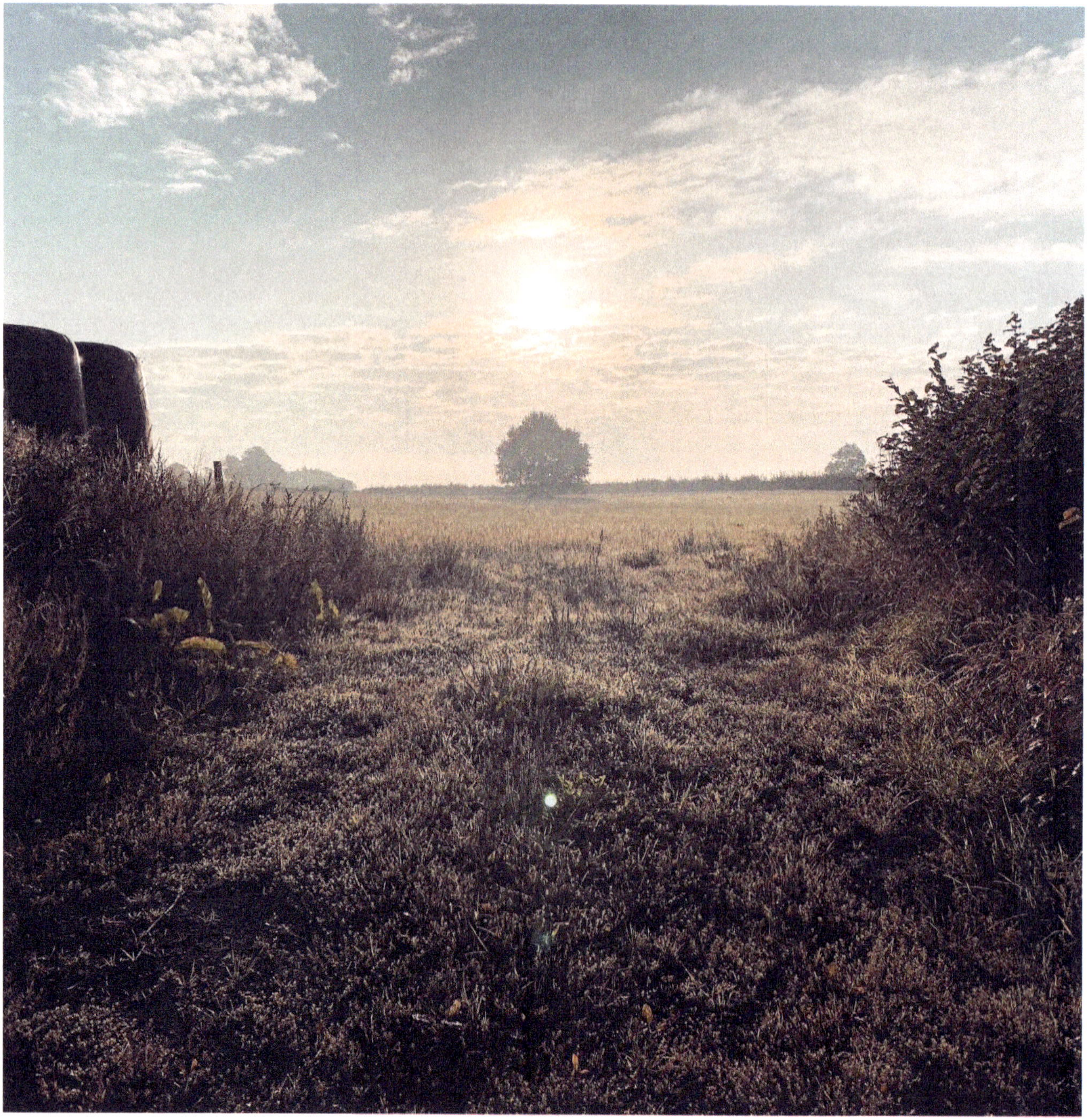

Once out of Shrewsbury, I was back onto the country lanes again. The sun was out, and I removed my layers one by one. Today I would be going over the Shropshire Hills which I had been warned about. But my feet were feeling much better after sorting them out earlier, and I was back to feeling positive again. I had a few more visitors show up as the morning turned to afternoon and once again, their support gave me energy. The flat roads turned to steep, hilly lanes and I pushed the jogger up and up, my arms stretched out like superman. Then I held on tightly when we went down the other side. The only thing that annoyed me were all the damn flies, they just would not leave me alone. But it had been a while since my last shower, so I guess I couldn't really blame them.

Once over the serious hills and back on some flatter terrain, I started to run again. At one point I found myself on a quiet lane alongside a field of cows. I said hello as I always did, and to my surprise and delight they rushed over to see me. I stopped and they stopped. When I ran, they ran. This went on for a little while until the road started to rise up to another hill, and it seemed that they had reached their limit. Apparently, cows don't run up hills and I couldn't blame them. I said goodbye and trotted on.

I was headed to Ludlow that evening, where another Double Brutal finisher, Lee, was waiting for me. I had met Lee the previous year in Llanberis when he had completed the race. My feet were starting to complain, so I checked my navigation app to see how far I had to go. A few miles later, I saw someone running towards me and to my relief, it was Lee. I was almost at 40 miles and I needed to stop soon. Lee ran his local leisure centre and said it wasn't too far away; I could camp on the grass area next to the car park if I wanted to.

We arrived at the centre and Lee unlocked the doors. He showed me to the kitchen area and after using the toilets (always a treat), we sat together and he made me hot chicken soup and multiple cups of tea. We chatted and laughed over his experiences at The Brutal and my adventures as I travelled down the UK. I truly loved these random encounters with people that Brutal had bought into my life.

After giving me a bag of goodies and showing me where I could pitch my tent, Lee left me to go home while I sorted out my kit and got into my sleeping bag. It was very cold again and I was wearing everything I had to try and keep warm. I decided to try and buy another sleeping bag when I got to Hereford, as it would be very difficult to finish if the cold kept robbing me of my sleep.

Day 17: Tuesday 1st September
Ludlow to Hereford - 26.71 miles - Total mileage: 623.09

The next morning, tired from another cold, sleepless night, I explained to Kathi and Gavin via the basecamp messenger group that I needed another sleeping bag. Kathi then went on to tell me that she had dreamt last night that Rab, our friend that had passed away the previous year, had visited her in her dreams and said that I had needed to buy an 'orange sleeping bag'. He had also gone on to talk about men's urinals, which had confused her a little. We laughed about it and caught Gavin up on how funny our friend had been and how much we missed him.

I allowed myself a few tears, as it was easier to let them out then fight the emotions. The sleepless nights were definitely pulling me down, but today I was headed for Hereford and a Premier Inn. It was another short day, at just over a marathon. I was obviously giving myself the usual hard time over this, but I needed to get some sleep and a good meal. And a damn good wash!

A little further down the road, a couple of rabbits burst out of the hedgerow, having a massive scrap. They were rolling over and over, fur flying. I automatically went into Cat Mum Mode and shouted at them to "pack it in, the pair of you!" They completely ignored me and raced off to fight some more while I shook my head, more concerned over the fact that I had just reprimanded the local wildlife.

Ludlow is a beautiful little town, but it was too early for any shops to be open yet. I ran on, heading to Leominster (which I still can't pronounce properly) with my music on to keep my pace up. I was motivated to get to Hereford as soon as possible, so I could make the most of my short day. I was looking forward to getting an actual hot meal in a restaurant, and I had been thinking about lasagne for most of the morning.

At about mile 12 I made it to Leominster (Leomin… LEM-*STUH*!!) and headed straight for a coffee shop.

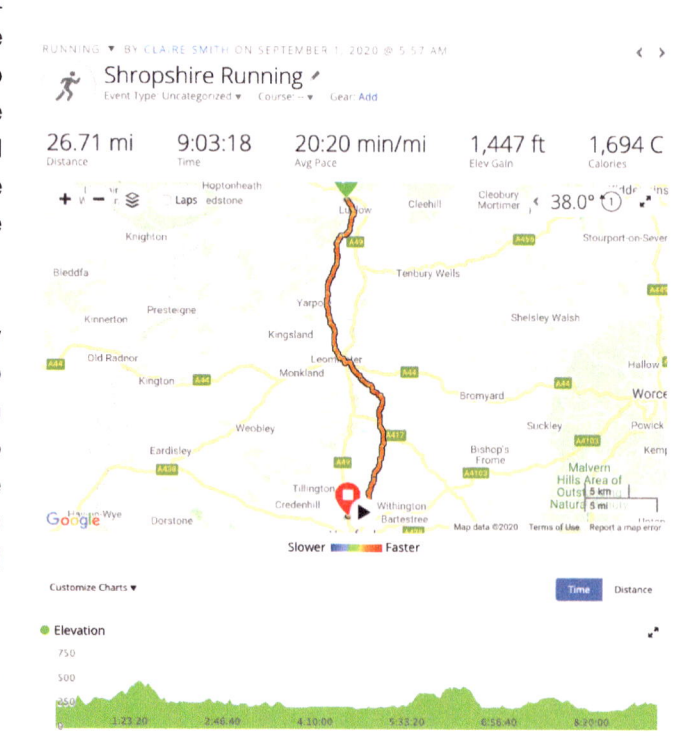

Once again I became the freak with the pushchair, so I sat self-consciously by the door, not making eye contact with anyone. I massively over ordered a huge almond croissant and giant slab of lemon cake alongside my large latte, and then had to ask for a serviette to take some of my leftovers away.

After escaping from the shop (balancing a cake on my dry bag and struggling with the door while everyone watched me), my phone rang. It was Radio Shropshire, asking if I would be available for an interview this morning. I agreed without giving it too much thought. Back home this would have made me fairly anxious, but the JOGLE experience had altered me and talking to strangers was now a normal part of life.

I found myself on a quiet, narrow lane. The sun was out and I was actually quite hot, a welcome but unfamiliar feeling. I peeled off some layers and reminded myself to drink more today (which I obviously forgot instantly). A lady who had taken part in the Half Brutal Triathlon turned up with her young children, all on bikes, to say hello. After they left, another woman who introduced herself as Fiona arrived to spend a little time with me. We got on well and chatted easily about our running ambitions. She was chasing the sub 3-hour marathon goal (something I could never aspire to) and it was interesting to hear about her experiences.

Just as Fiona was saying goodbye, another friend, Pete, who I had met at a Lanzarote Swimming Camp back in January, appeared on his huge fat bike, the massive tyres making me laugh. We chatted awhile and I mentioned how cold the last few nights had been. Pete asked if I wanted another sleeping bag, as he had loads at home. I gratefully said yes, and he promised to find me the next day.

Pete left and I was on my own again. I reached for the almond croissant and was just about to stuff a huge piece in my mouth when the phone rang. It was the radio interview I had completely forgotten about. The producer put me on hold whilst Ronan Keeting sang about life being a rollercoaster. The song was very appropriate and made me laugh. The music ended and the DJ started to introduce me and explain what I was doing to the listeners. We chatted easily for a few minutes, laughing about the adventures I had been having along the way. Then he was gone, and another song was playing.

I was left in peace to eat my croissant. Looking on my navigation app, I saw I had about six miles left to get to Hereford. Six miles… my feet had started to throb quite early that day, it was like they knew it was a short one and didn't want me to miss out on the intense pain normally felt nearer the 40 mile target. By the time I walked down the road that lead to the hotel, I was in bits. Once in the room, I lay on the bed and took a deep breath as the pain receded a little. It was mid-afternoon and I had a good few hours to sort myself out and walk the short distance to Halfords to pick up a few things I needed.

After I had sorted myself out and made myself look less bag lady-ish, I made my way out of the hotel. I limped along the pavement, my legs and feet still really sore. I had a weird feeling, like I had forgotten something important. After a second or two, I realised that I didn't have the buggy! I was a little shocked at how odd I felt without it. How would it be when I finally finished? Would I need little buggy runs around the block when I got back home to ween myself off it?

Once I had got what I needed, I hobbled back to the Premier Inn and made my way to the restaurant. The waitress showed me to my table and to my delight, there was lasagne on the menu. I ordered an apple and mango juice and waited for my food. My feet throbbed away to themselves under the table and I slipped off my flip-flops. I looked around and wondered if the family sat opposite would notice if I rubbed them a little… It wasn't really the normal thing to do in a restaurant, but then nothing I was doing at the moment was normal. I tried not to make any weird 'When Harry Met Sally" faces as I massaged them, but it was hard.

The lasagne and thick cut chips hit the spot. Back in the hotel room again, I lay on my bed and felt sleepy. Not the best day in terms of mileage, but a decent meal, bath and warm, comfy bed was much needed tonight. I set my alarm for 4:00am and fell asleep almost instantly.

FNC 228 T
GB
CYM
IF YOU THINK THIS IS SLOW WAIT UNTIL WE GO UPHILL!
F
B
D
CZ
PL
LT
LV
S
NL
CYMRU AM BYTH
MICHELIN

Day 18: Wednesday 2nd September
Hereford to Aust (Severn Bridge) - 40.83 miles - Total mileage: 663.92

It was still dark when I left the hotel, but all the street lights were on in the city so a head torch wasn't needed. Once I started moving, I felt the benefits of an early night and a full eight hours of sleep in the warm. My head was in a good place, as the night before Gavin had told me I would cross the Severn Bridge this evening. Initially I had thought he was joking; surely there was no way I had made it to that point already. But he confirmed that if I covered 40 miles today, I would make it across. I doubted this would be quite as exciting as a night crossing of the Forth Bridge, but it was still a great goal to focus on today when things got tough.

Once through Hereford I enjoyed a gorgeous sunrise on the quiet country lanes. I passed a cottage with a box of free apples for anyone who wanted one. I took three and ate one as I walked, enjoying the sweetness of the fruit and feeling content. Pete (who I had seen the previous day) arrived, this time in his Land Rover rather than on a fat bike, and handed me a sleeping bag. I gratefully stowed it away for later, thanking him for taking the time to come and find me.

I hit the half marathon point at mid-morning and stopped for 10 minutes to raise my feet and eat something. Despite some big hills, I was making good progress today and hoped tonight's finish wouldn't be too late. Back on lanes that had become a little flatter, I started to run. Then suddenly I heard a strange snapping, crunching noise, and I watched as the right-side back wheel slowly rolled away from me and the rest of the jogger.

It was a sightly surreal moment. I held up the buggy and looked at the wheel that had been under my hands one minute, and the next was lying on the other side of the road. I can't say that I hadn't been expecting it because I had, but it was still a bit of a shock.

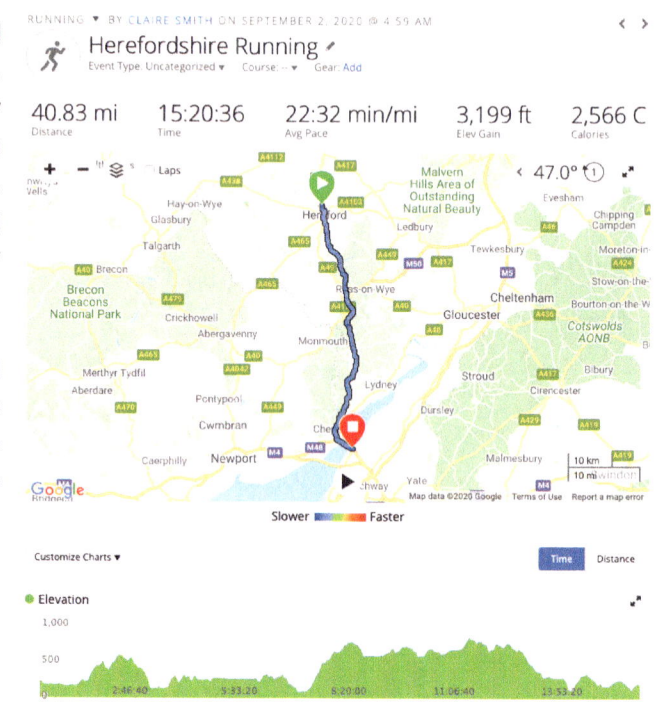

I lay the jogger on its side and inspected the damage. The long bolt thingy that runs all the way through the hub of the wheel (apparently the technical name for this is an "axle") had sheered clean off, and even I knew that only some serious maintenance could sort it out. I looked ahead of me and saw some farm buildings a few 100 metres down the road. Picking up the buggy and grabbing the runaway wheel, I struggled towards them, hoping there would be someone there who could help me.

Once outside I could see that it was more than just a farm, with a sizeable industrial unit opposite the barns. I dumped the buggy in the driveway and walked up to the reception. I was greeted by a large golden retriever, which in my opinion is what every company should have as their receptionist. As I was saying hello to the friendly dog, an older man appeared. He told the dog off for blatantly breaking COVID-19 rules, and I felt bad that I had encouraged it. He then turned to me with a slightly annoyed and confused look on his face.

"What can I do for you?" He asked. I tried to explain what I was doing and what had just happened, but I only seemed to make him more annoyed and confused. "You've broken your bike?" he asked me, frowning. "Sort of..." I replied. "Can I show you?" I thought it might make more sense if he saw the buggy.

"You've come from Scotland with *this*?" He looked at me in disbelief. "Erm, yes" I confirmed. "And I need to get to Land's End. But this has happened" I held up the wheel. That seemed to do the trick. His face softened a little and he said, "Let me make a phone call." The man disappeared back to the office, calling his dog to follow him. After a few moments, he returned and said that someone would be along to help me soon. And with that, he turned and walked away.

After a few minutes, a man in coveralls appeared with the same slightly confused look on his face. I pointed to the jogger and held up the wheel again, feeling a little foolish. "Ah, okay. Follow me." We crossed over the road and the man told me to lay the buggy down outside one of the big barns as he unlocked it and pulled the door open. Inside was an impressive and organised workshop. I allowed myself to feel hopeful that something in there would fix the jogger, at least in the short term.

The man got to work while I sat outside the barn on the concrete. Messaging basecamp to let Gavin and Kathi know what was going on, I also updated social media with what had happened. My mum texted me asking why I had stopped, and I explained how a wheel had fallen off the buggy, but a farmer was helping to fix it.

After about 30 minutes, the buggy was upright again. A set of bolts on a piece of threaded bar now replaced the old axle, which the man had put in a bag for me. "You might need this if you have to get another one, in case the left one goes" he said. I had already been worrying about the same thing and gratefully put the broken axle down the side of my dry bag, wondering if I would go past a bike shop later. The fact that the baby jogger wasn't actually a bike concerned me a little (I later found out that I had been amazingly lucky to break down so close

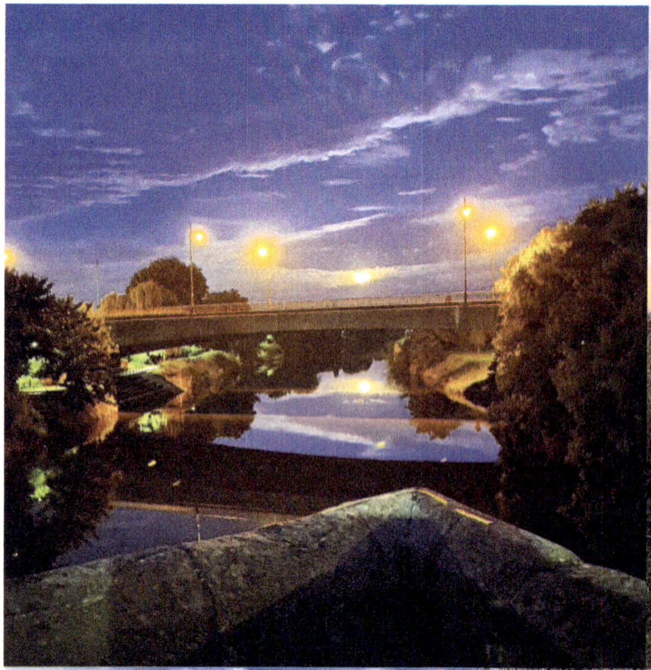

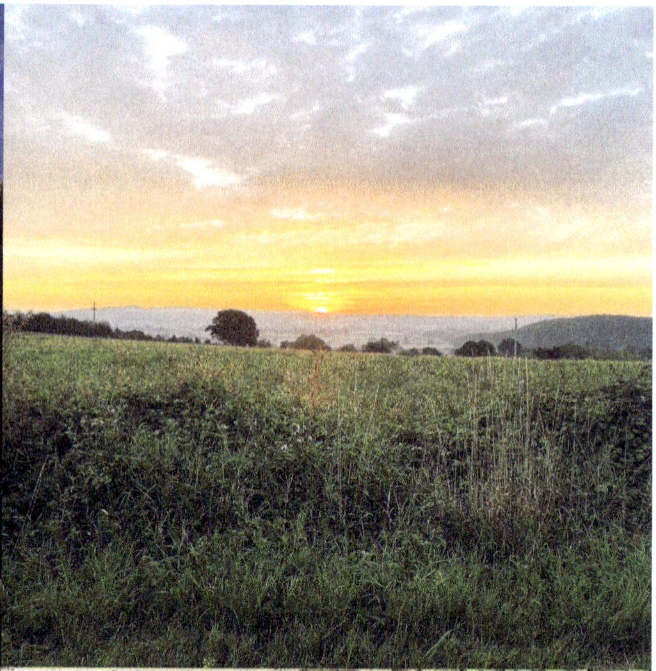

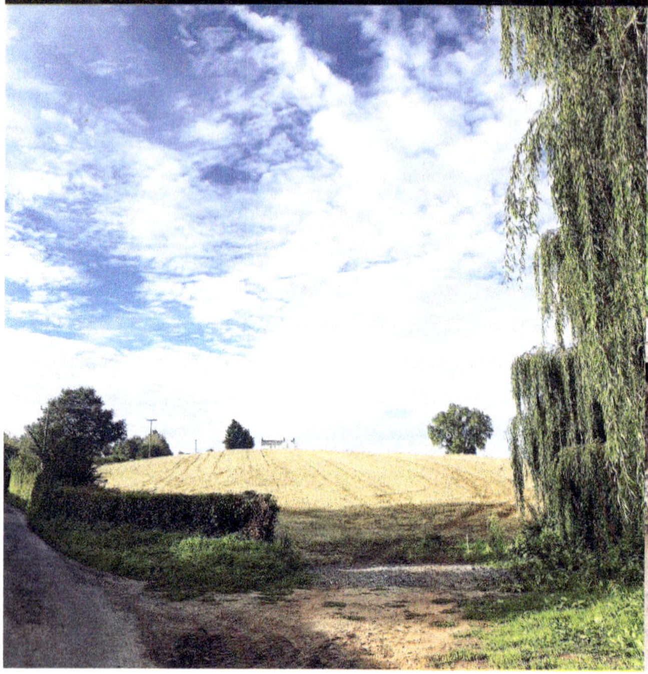

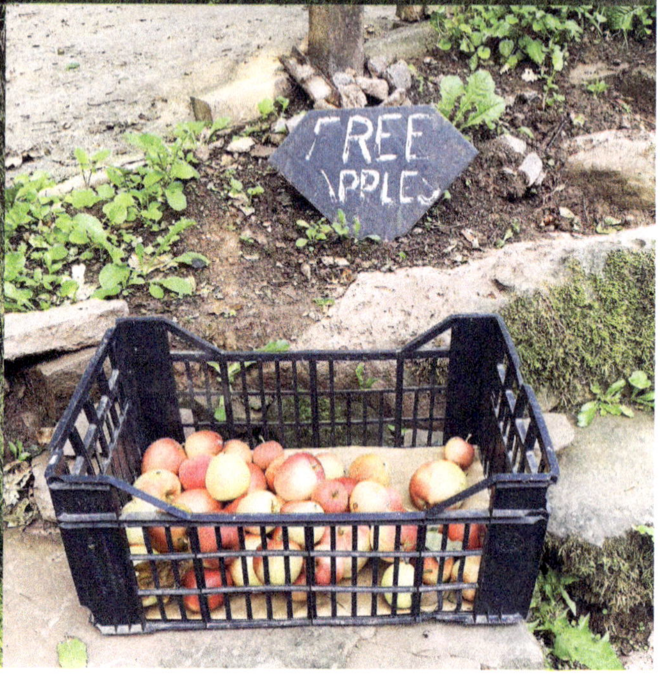
FREE
PPLES

to a workshop that could make bespoke parts; a replacement axle for the baby jogger would have been almost impossible to buy on route).

I thanked the man about 10 times. I actually wanted to give him a massive hug for basically saving me hours (if not days) of stress and hassle, but he was a quiet, reserved man and I felt the last thing he wanted was some random woman leaping on him. Also, in these strange times of COVID-19, I shouldn't be hugging anyone at all. I settled on thanking him a few more times. Aware that I was starting to sound like a lunatic, I finally forced myself to stop talking and left the man in peace.

Back on the road again, I reflected on what had just happened. I was bowled over by the kindness of total strangers, and I was experiencing so much of this on my adventure down the UK. Yes, there were a few idiots out there, but mostly people wanted to get involved and help me if they could. It also struck me just how calm I had remained over the last hour. I had barely reacted at all. Compare that to the first puncture back on the Scottish/English border, where I'd practically had a breakdown on the garage forecourt…

I made my way up some ridiculously steep hills near Symonds Yat (the kind of climbs where I have to stretch my body out almost parallel with the road, like I'm flying), pushing the buggy ever onwards. The sunny morning gave way to drizzle and as I got to the top of yet another hill, I looked up to see someone waiting for me. The man introduced himself as Nick and asked if I wanted some company for a little while. The conversation came easily as we chatted about open water swimming and how we had trained throughout the lockdown period.

After a while we came to a small village. I picked up some supplies and Nick offered to get me a hot drink so I could sit and have a break. Once he'd returned and I sat enjoying a proper coffee, he said he could go back to his garage and find some bolts so I would have spares in case I had a repeat of the wheel failure he'd seen on Instagram earlier. I was yet again stunned by the kindness of people I'd never met, going out of their way to help me on this journey. I thanked him and handed him the bag with the broken axle, and he promised to find me later that day.

Before Nick left, he warned me that my route was about to get tough. I had miles and miles of a fast, busy B road coming up, and there were no alternatives unless I was prepared to make a massive detour. I thanked him for the heads-up. As the rain started to pour down, I braced myself for a hard afternoon.

The road did not disappoint, and soon my good mood had been replaced by a pointless anger at the cars and lorries that raced past me, soaking me with the large puddles that had now formed. The faster and closer they got to me, the angrier I became. I knew it was a waste of precious energy and I tried not to care, but it was almost impossible as another large Audi brushed past my elbow at 70 mph.

Halfway through my afternoon from hell, just as I was going up another hill, I heard a voice behind me. Turning around I saw a lady running up to me. "Would you like a cup of tea?" she asked. I was a little confused, but I am physically unable to turn down a cuppa at any time, so I said "yes, that would be lovely". The lady then explained that she owned the campsite on the other side of the road, and they had seen me earlier when they drove past. I followed her to the entrance of the site, and she disappeared for a few minutes. She then reappeared holding a cardboard cup of lovely, hot tea. I gladly took it as rain dripped off my hood and ran down my back. I thanked her, so grateful for this small act of kindness during an afternoon where nobody on the road seemed to care about me at all.

As I continued on, so did the rain. A visit from some members of my awesome Brutal Crew, Matt and Karen, lifted my spirits and we stood in a lay-by laughing about the crazy things I did and how I always seemed to attract the worst weather, even during what was supposed to be summer. After they got back into their warm, dry van, I was on my own again. I put my head down and pushed on to Chepstow.

As I made it to the outskirts of town, I finally found some pavement. The relief of getting off the roads during rush hour was immense. Soon after I had yet another visitor, this time a previous Triple Brutal and DecaUK finisher, Will Denny. Will is a great endurance athlete and all-round lovely guy. He had a boot full of goodies and I took some much needed Compeed and Lucozade, as I hadn't eaten as much as I should have done that day and my blood sugar levels were falling. He asked if I wanted a coffee and I replied that a latte would be brilliant. He disappeared off to find a coffee shop.

Will soon returned with a large and very welcome Starbucks and I gulped it down, needing the energy. At last the Severn Bridge came into view and my spirits rose. A few more miles and I would be across it, another milestone ticked off.

Once I arrived and the rain had finally stopped, I pulled out my phone and took some pictures of the impressive suspension bridge than crossed the River Severn. Sending the photos to Gavin and Kathi, while they messaged their whoops of support, I started to get an uneasy feeling. Where were all the cars, I wondered. My heart sank - was the bridge closed? What would I do if it was? There was another bridge far off in the distance, but the thought of more miles at this point was devastating.

At that moment, a group of three women power-walked past me so I called over to them. "Excuse me, do you know why there's nobody on the bridge?" One of the women confirmed that it was closed tonight, but only to traffic. "We can still cross it," she smiled at me. I breathed a massive sigh of relief and almost sprinted onto the bridge, as if I had to cross within a time limit. After calming down a little, I slowed up to enjoy the views across the vast expanse of water. Without the noise of traffic, all I could hear was the wind.

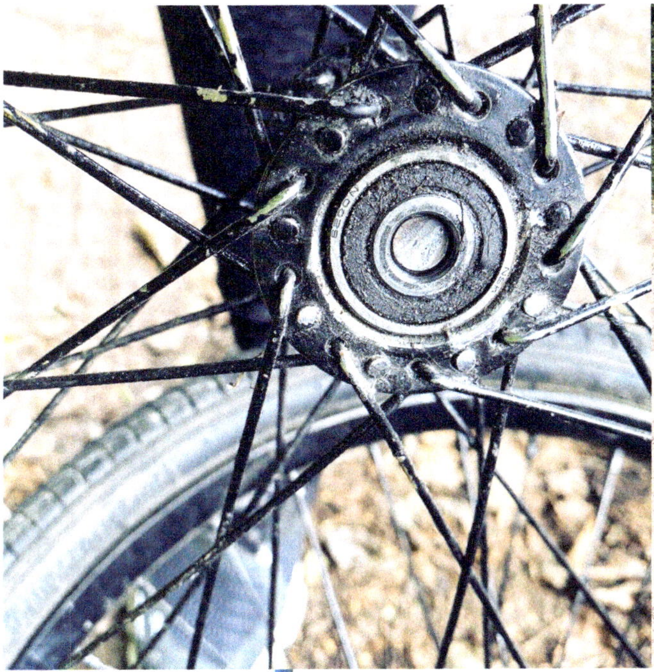

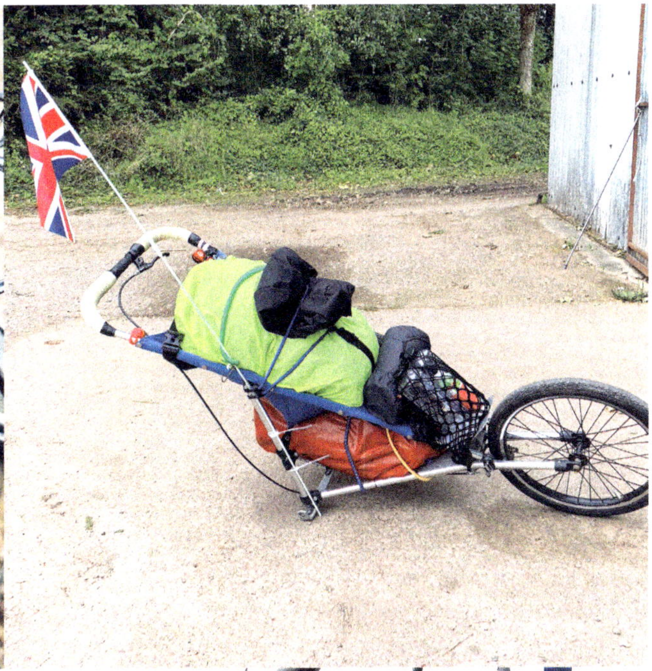

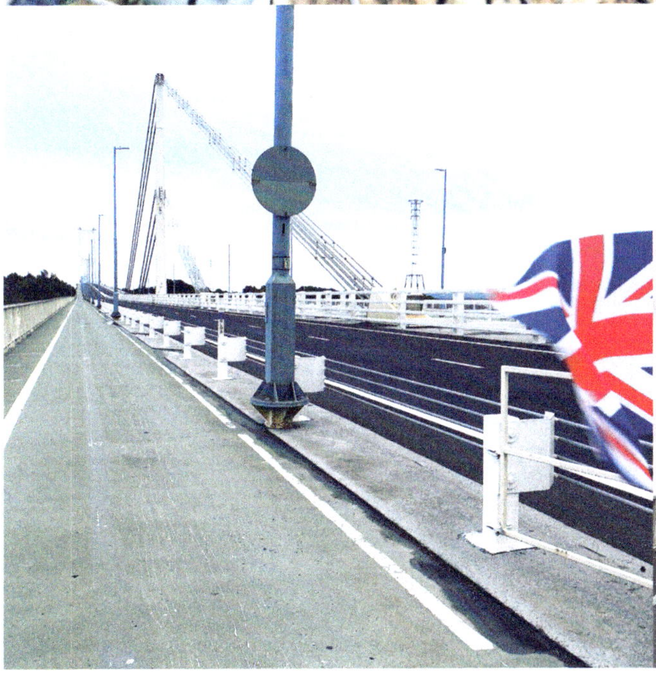

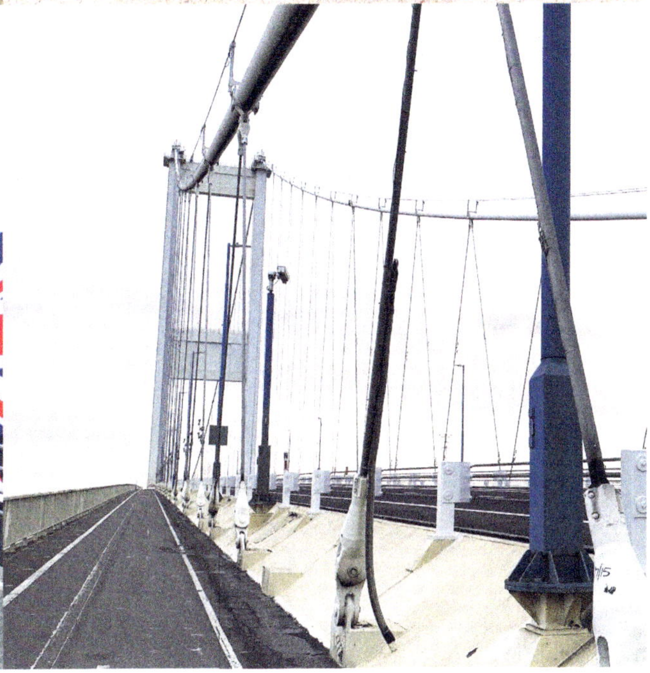

As the end of the bridge came into sight, the sun was setting and thoughts of where I would sleep for the night were on my mind. I had planned to camp, but Gavin and a few others had said how hard that would be, as it was very built up and there was a definite lack of fields over the next few miles. Then my phone rang – it was my friend Matthew, who was keeping an eye on me via the tracker. He informed me that I was literally about to walk past a Travel Lodge, and there were rooms available. After 40 long miles of buggy breakages, mega hills, heavy rain and a lot of close calls with cars and lorries, I didn't need an excuse to forgo wild camping in return for another night in a warm, cosy bed. As I walked, Matthew gave me some more news. He told me that he'd looked into the current self-supported Fastest Known Time for John o' Groats to Land's End and couldn't find anything about an official record. "I'm not saying someone hasn't completed it in 17 days, but I can't see anything online that recognises it as the official time. In fact, I can't find *any* official time for the FKT. Two guys made an attempt in 2018, but both abandoned. What I'm saying is, if you can finish this thing, you'll be the record holder."

I wasn't sure how I felt about that. In my mind I'd fallen behind record pace early on in the challenge, and since then I'd only been thinking about completing it. I was also pretty sure that keyboard adventurers would be quick to say I'd received a lot of help along the way, so my attempt wasn't really self-supported. For me, the point of the JOGLE was to test my limits and raise some money for charity in the process. I didn't need to explain myself or justify how I did it to anyone, so if getting the FKT would attract that kind of attention then I could do without it. "Well, according to FKT rules it doesn't actually matter if people help you, as long as it isn't pre-arranged" Matthew said. "You've provided a link to real-time tracking, you've got GPX files of your route, and you're posting daily updates and photos on the internet. Like it or not, when you finish, you're getting that FKT," he said with a laugh.

Day 19: Thursday 3rd September
Aust (Severn Bridge) to Rooks Bridge - 39.5 miles - Total mileage: 703.42

The day started badly. I *always* have massive issues getting in and out of motorway services and I wasn't going to let the fact I wasn't in a car stop me from going around in total confusion for a full 30 minutes before I managed to escape. To be fair, I had made it out of the services themselves and I was now on a roundabout in the dark, whilst it poured with rain, trying and failing to find the correct exit. It wasn't helping that even at 5:00am it was already heaving with traffic. "I'm not dying on a bloody roundabout on the M48" I muttered to myself, as yet another lorry narrowly missed me, spraying me with water.

Finally, I managed to escape the chaos of the traffic and breathed a sigh of relief as I turned on to a quiet road leading to a cycle path. At least it was still too early for anyone to be watching me on the tracker yet, I thought (I later found that actually a few people had been watching and wondering what on earth I had been up to). I tried to put it behind me and headed towards the river. I came to a large "Road Closed' sign on my left and stopped. I checked my navigation app and saw that apart from a dual carriageway, there was no other option. I just hoped that the road was only closed to traffic, not a mildly unhinged woman with a baby jogger.

The road was very closed. High Haras fencing barricaded the entrance and the only other way around it was an extremely narrow V-shaped gate that I didn't even attempt to get the buggy through. I put my head on the handlebar and tried not to cry. It was 6:00am and I was barely two miles away from where I had started an hour ago. I may as well have stayed in bed…

I turned back and headed towards the duel carriageway, messaging basecamp as I moved along the road. Kathi tried to find an alternative route for me, but there was nothing. I had no choice but to get onto the verge. For two miles, I pushed the buggy over thick grass with rocks and ruts jamming up against the wheels, making me swear and stress about the other wheels breaking. The traffic was fast and unrelenting, and the wind and rain added to what was turning out to be a really, really bad morning. "Stay positive, stay positive, stay positive" I said to myself, over and over, determined to not let this break me.

Once I was free of the dreaded verge and back on pavements, I found myself going through a small town. I tried to eat something to get my energy levels up, hoping in turn it would help with my mental state. I felt horrible and really low. Pissed off with myself for wasting time and precious miles. And also concerned that my feet were soaking wet and already really painful. It was barely 10:00am.

I was trudging along feeling more than a little sorry for myself, when Rob, my Brutal Events water safety guy messaged me saying he was trying to track me down as he had a coffee for me. He told me to stay put, and I took the opportunity to sort my feet out. There was nowhere to shelter from the rain and as I was soaked through anyway, I just plonked myself down on the pavement and pulled off my shoes and socks. My feet were an absolute state. Soggy Compeed and bits of skin hung off them. Just at that moment Rob showed up holding some Starbucks cups. He looked at me and raised his eyebrows. "You look happy" he said smirking slightly. I glared at him, told him to bugger off, and then stood up and gave him a huge hug. I didn't have to hide my feelings with Rob as he was a core part of my crew who had seen me in varying states of distress over the years.

After Rob left, I managed to escape from the town and back onto some quieter roads. The rain eased up and then finally stopped, and the sun came out. I rounded a corner and saw a bearded man with an excitable dog waiting for me. After the terrible morning I had just had, I was thrilled to see Brutal mate Matt Pritchard and his lovely dog, Lemmy. He gave me a big hug and a bag of Twiglets and I bent down to pat Lemmy while he jumped and ran around us. Matt had completed my Double Brutal, Continuous Deca, and plenty of his own ultra-endurance events - including running from Land's End to John o' Groats (although he had the good sense to do it with a support crew). As a result, he really understood what I was going through.

After Matt and Lemmy went on with their day, I headed off with my mood much improved. More quiet lanes followed, and I started making some real progress. However, at about mile 24 I started to feel completely exhausted, the stress and weather having really taken a toll. Walking past a field, I decided that an hour's sleep now would help ensure I made it to the 40-mile mark later on. Pulling off the road, I found a corner of the field where I couldn't be seen by anyone, set up my tent and crawled inside.

An hour or so later, feeling much better after my rest, I cracked on with the afternoon. I was now on a bike trail called the Strawberry Line which meant miles of traffic-free running to enjoy. Putting my music on, I compared how I felt now to my mood earlier this morning. The highs and lows of ultra-endurance events were exhausting, but at least I was never bored!

A little while later my phone rang and my good friend and Brutal business partner, James, called me. We chatted away for a while about his work and what had happened to me that day, when he started asking some random questions about the path I was on and whether it was road or trail. It turned out that James was on the same path and was trying to surprise me with a visit, but as my tracker only updated every five minutes, he was having some issues. "Stay there" he instructed me, and after a few moments I saw his silver car at the end of the track. I waved at him madly, so happy to see him.

Once James found me, we spent about 10 minutes talking and laughing. He was shocked by my now obvious weight loss and was keen to see me eat some food whilst he was there. I happily munched on a sandwich. I loved seeing people on the route, but there was something about seeing my close friends that gave me such a huge buzz of energy. Before James left, he told me that the Brutal Squirrel (Justin) was also on his way to see me later that evening.

I was now back on some busier roads but still running and making good progress. As promised, Justin turned up, calling out support and waving from his van as he went past. He stopped further down the road and I sat for a while with him, rubbing my feet as they had started their normal painful throbbing. The afternoon turned into evening, so I pulled out my head torch and switched on the buggy lights. As it got darker, roots and overhanging bushes on the narrow pavement snagged the jogger, making progress harder.

At almost 40 miles I stopped in a lay-by and told Justin I was going to start looking for a place to sleep. He looked a little alarmed, as earlier we had agreed that I should try to get to a hotel further down the road. But that was still

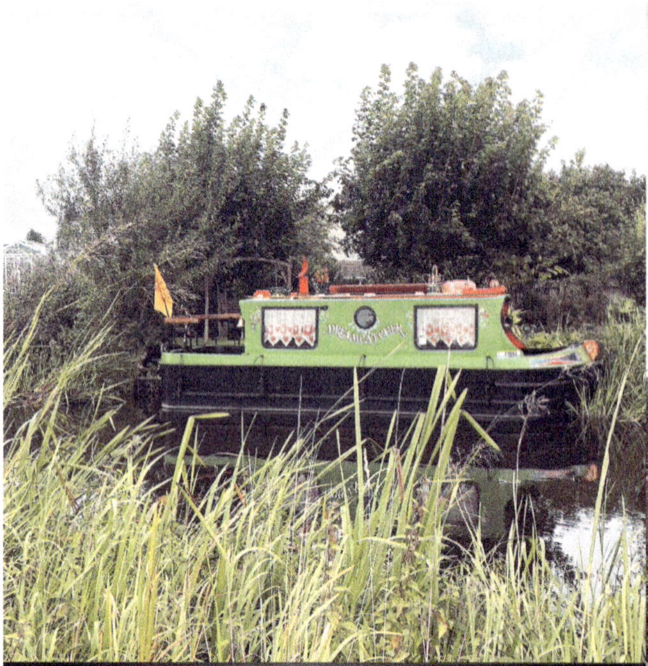
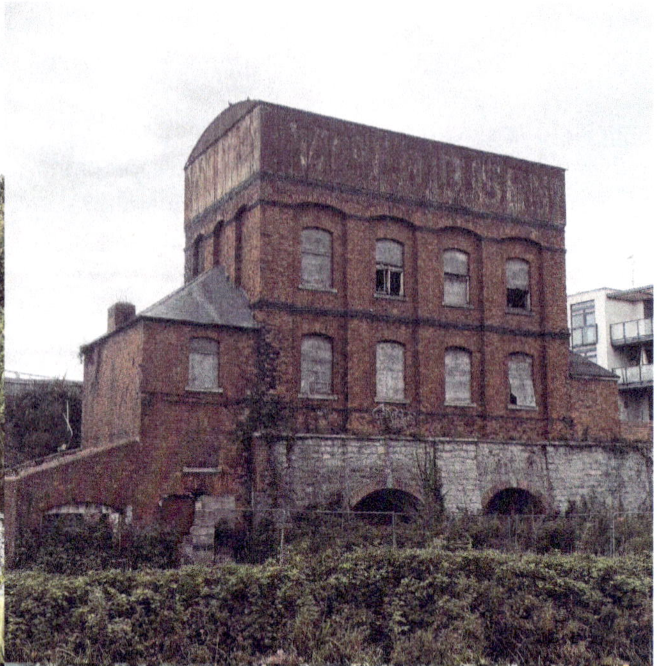
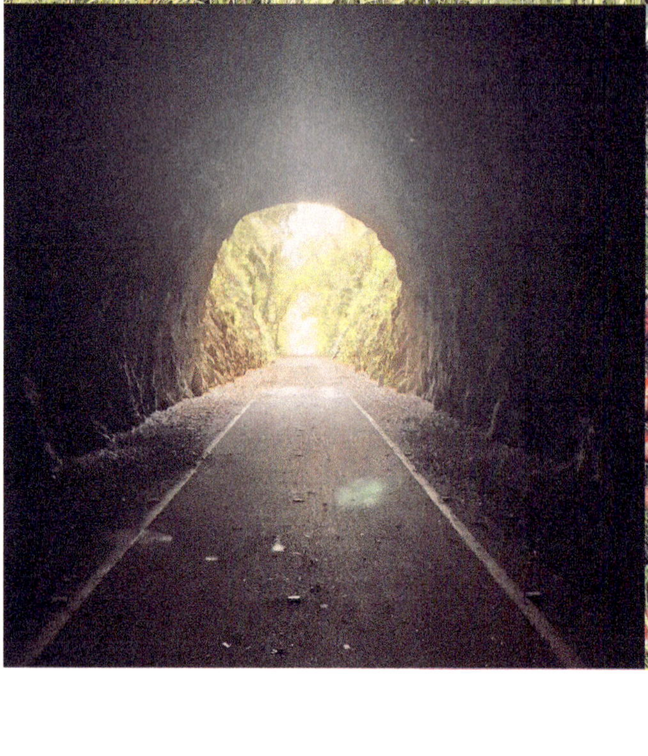
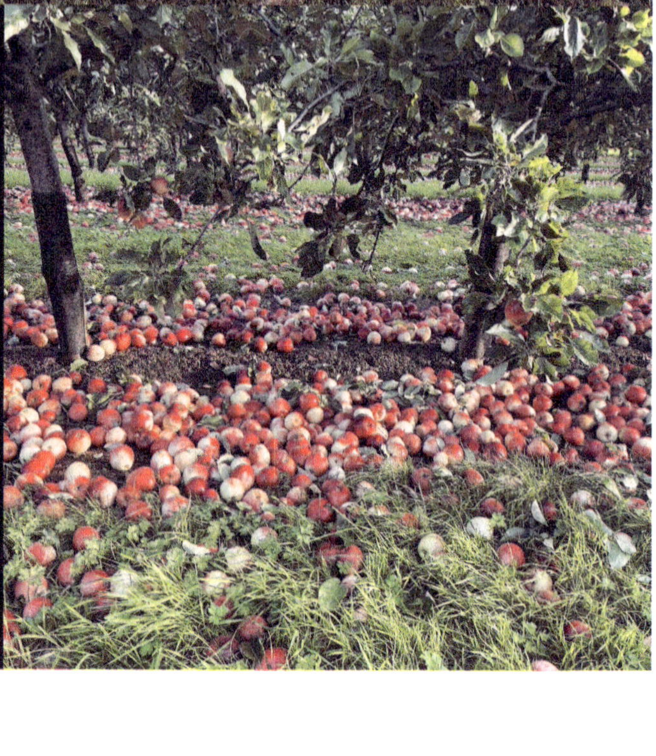

over four miles away, and I was shattered. I kept going along the busy road, looking desperately for somewhere to camp but there was nothing suitable.

Eventually I settled on a gateway to a field, set back off the road a little. Justin raised his eyebrows and asked if I was sure this was where I wanted to sleep, and I just shrugged. "I need to get off my feet, Justin" I said. He gave me a hug goodbye and left me to pitch my tent. Once I was inside, I sorted my kit and pulled out my sleeping bag. I was too tired to bother with cooking tonight, I just wanted to sleep. Just before I passed out, I noticed that the new sleeping bag Pete had given me was bright orange. I thought back to the dream Kathi had about Rab and smiled. Then I set my alarm for 4:00am and almost immediately fell asleep.

I awoke with a start. A bright light was shining into my tent and a man's voice was saying "come out and talk to me." I had been sleeping so deeply that for a moment I thought I was still dreaming. More torch light shone into my tent and the voice, this time much louder, commanded "come on out, now!" I realised that this was definitely not a dream, and with shaking hands I unzipped the tent door. The first thing I saw was a crowbar. Then I looked up and saw a man who didn't look as scary as he sounded, but he wasn't exactly smiling either. Keeping my eyes firmly on the crowbar, I tried to explain what I was doing. The man's look of anger turned to one of confusion before he asked me if I had been here the night before. Now it was my turn to be confused, as I replied that I had been crossing the Severn Bridge last night. I took a deep breath and tried to explain again what I was doing, and also apologise for camping on his land. The man then told me that he had been broken into the night before and had thought that I was part of the gang of thieves. I assured him that I was not a thief, I was just exhausted and hadn't been able to make it to a hotel.

Once we both fully understood each other's perspective, we were able to relax and even started laughing about how random the situation was. I apologised again and asked him if he wanted me to leave. "No, no of course not," he said. "In fact, can I help you at all? Take you to the hotel? Open the gate for you?" I replied that all I wanted was to get some sleep, and if he didn't mind me staying here, that would be perfect. "Absolutely," he replied. After a few more minutes of chatting, he went back to his house and I tried going back to sleep. But as I zipped my tent back up, I remembered what the man had said about thieves breaking in the night before. For the next few hours I just lay there, desperate for sleep but unable to relax.

For the first time since leaving John o' Groats, I felt scared to be alone in the darkness.

Day 20: Friday 4th September

Rooks Bridge to Great Fossend - 40.5 miles - **Total mileage: 743.92**

In the early hours of Friday morning I gave up trying to sleep and decided I might as well be getting some miles done. I got up and packed the tent away, wishing it was light but knowing it would be hours before sunrise. Once I was away from the streets, I found myself on some dark and very quiet lanes. Still spooked from the night before, I put my audio book on to try a distract myself. It was funny how I'd covered over 700 miles through Scotland and most of the UK and felt safe, but now I was checking behind me as I walked.

The dark lanes went on and on, but eventually the sun rose and I found myself next to the M5. People were now up and driving to work as I made my way across the roundabout (this was always fun) and into a large, newly built service station. I had covered 10 miles and it was only about 7:00am, but I suddenly felt ravenously hungry. I popped into the shop and bought myself a pain au chocolate, sausage roll and a large latte. Sitting outside, I devoured my very unhealthy breakfast and once finished, refilled my water bottles and CamelBak before setting off again.

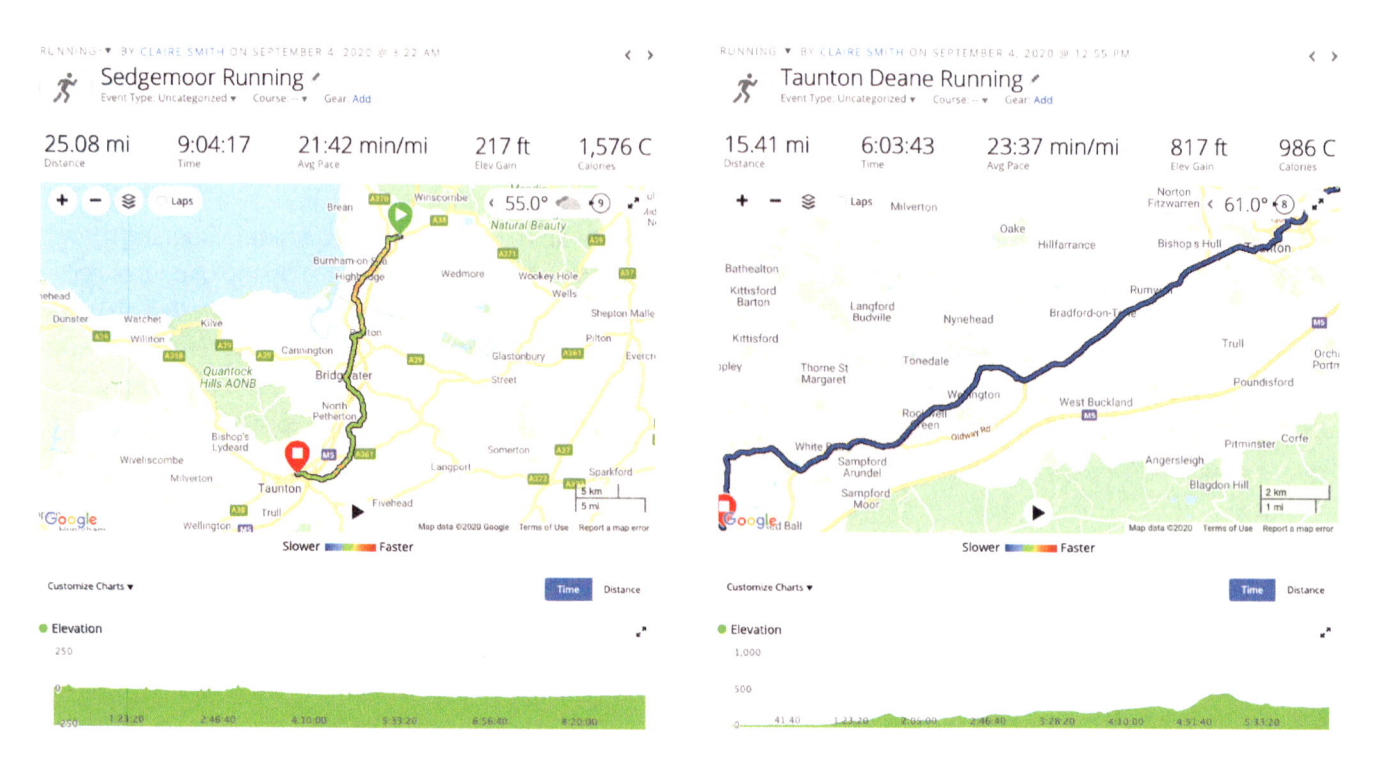

I made my way through Bridgwater, busy with people and cars. Thankfully, after a few miles I found myself on a quiet canal path that I would stay on for the next 14 miles. This was good and bad news. Good, because it was a gorgeous traffic-free path with amazing wildlife and scenery to keep me distracted. Bad, because the path was covered in stones and very uneven. This made the going hard work for the buggy and stressed me a little over concerns of wheels or other parts breaking. But there was nothing to be done about it. If it happens, it happens and I'll just have to deal with it, I thought. I made the decision to enjoy the day and put worries out of my mind.

As I got to mile 25 I began to feel really sleepy. Hardly surprising, considering I had only slept for two hours and had covered the best part of a marathon already today. The canal path was lovely, but there was nowhere to rest away from the walkers and their dogs. I pulled off the path onto a patch of grass and spread my coat out. After eating a little, I tried to sleep. But just as I was drifting off, large drops of rain started splashing onto my face. Even though I was exhausted, lying in the rain was just plain stupid.

Fifteen minutes off my feet had helped though, and I went in search of a garage for more food and coffee. Once my energy levels were up, I was able to get more miles under my belt. The day went on as the scenery changed from canal path to the bustling town of Taunton. More busy roads and another large town, then finally back on quiet country lanes again. I chatted to Kathi and Gavin in the basecamp group as I walked to distract me from the ever-increasing pain in my feet and legs. Apparently, Kathi's daughter was thinking about getting a Chihuahua called Paddy who looked like a reincarnated Latino pop star. That did the trick.

As day turned to evening and I got closer to the 40-mile mark, I checked the map. My route was soon to take me back on the canal path and as I had already tried (and failed) to sleep on it today, I didn't fancy trying to camp on it tonight. I needed to find somewhere in the next quarter mile, or I would have to go back on myself. I found a field with a gate that was loosely tied with string and decided to sneak in. It was still light, which made me nervous, but by this point I was desperate for somewhere to sleep. Once in the field I found a corner and stood back to check my surroundings. My heart sank, there were cows on the far side of the field. Frustratingly, in my haste to find somewhere I had not noticed this. Camping with sheep was one thing, but cows? I had visions of them curiously inspecting the tent, and then trampling me to death in the middle of the night. All things considered, I decided I should find somewhere less risky.

However, every field I came to had a locked gate and I realised I was out of options when I arrived at the canal path. I looked to my left and saw a few houses leading to a small village. Could I knock on some doors and ask if anyone minded if I camped in their garden, I wondered? The rain had started to fall again, and I noticed I had yet another puncture. Perfect timing. I let out a long, slow breath. I was so tired. I pushed the jogger past a few houses and then found myself at the entrance to a school. There was nobody about, so I wandered across the playground and made my way to the bike sheds so I would have some shelter while I changed the inner tube. Once I'd fixed the flat tyre, I decided to cook some food as I was out of the rain and waiting for it to get dark.

It seemed to take forever for the sun to set while I sat and ate my pasta, but as I waited a thought occurred to me. I could just stay here, in the bike shed. I was out of sight from people and sheltered from the rain, too. I was a little uneasy about the decision, but as I didn't have many options at that point, I decided to set up my tent. Once I'd crawled inside, I pulled out my bedding and lay down to sleep. I felt slightly apprehensive about camping in a school, but I was so exhausted I soon dropped off.

I woke suddenly to the sound of a metal gate being closed followed by a chain rattling. My heart sank at the realisation that I was now locked in an infant school. "Awesome work, Claire" I said to myself. After a few minutes I poked my head out of the tent and looked across at the main gates. From the street lights I could just make out their height in the darkness. Although the situation was far from ideal, I thought that I should be able to climb them when I needed to get out in the morning. Getting the buggy over would be another story, but it wasn't like I had a choice. I went back into my tent for yet another very uneasy night.

Day 21: Saturday 5th September
Great Fossend to Okehampton - 44.7 miles - **Total mileage: 788.62**

After what felt like about two hours of anxious and broken sleep, I got up and quietly packed up. Wheeling the buggy across the playground I looked around, hoping there were no insomniac dog walkers about. Once I was at the gate, I unloaded the buggy and dropped the bags over the other side. I then awkwardly lifted the jogger over, doing my best not to damage it when it landed on the pavement. Then it was my turn. Jamming my foot on the metal hinge and lifting my stiff leg over the gate, I jumped down the other side to land on my mangled feet. Not very graceful, but I was more concerned that nobody was watching me while simultaneously phoning the police.

Once I had escaped the school and hastily repacked the buggy, I promised myself that I would never sleep in a school again. It had been a really stupid idea and definitely not worth the stress. At least I hadn't been caught; I'm sure I could have explained my way out of trouble like I did with the crowbar wielding farmer, but it would not have been fun. After a few minutes walk, I was back on the canal path where I breathed a big sigh of relief.

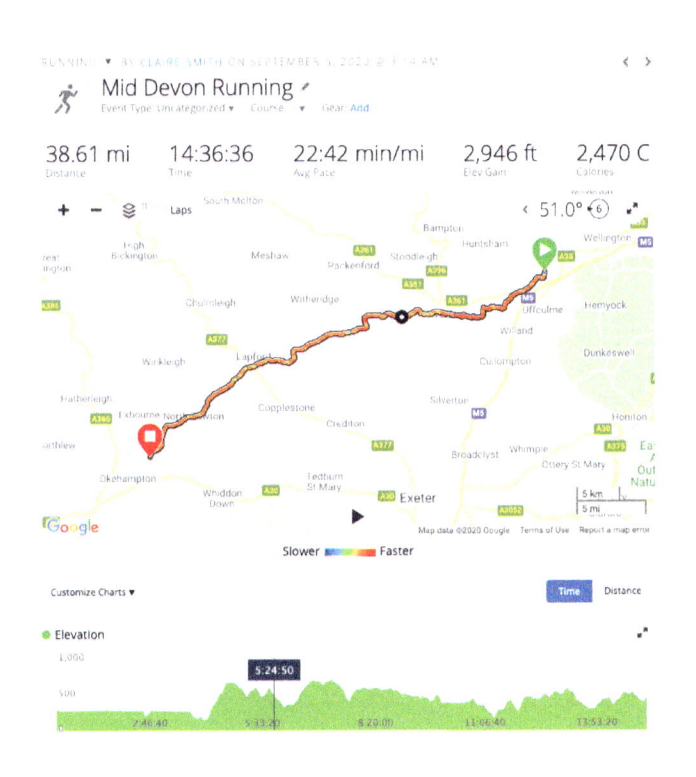

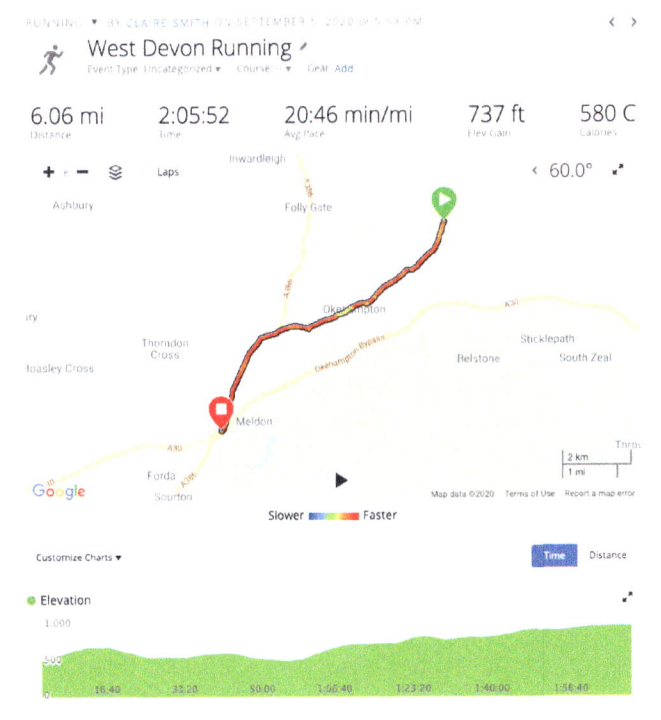

It was just after 3:00am and still pitch black. I pulled my head torch from the essentials bag that hung from my handlebars and switched it on. I had several miles of gravel path to cover, so progress would be steady but a little slow this morning. A few hours in, while I was eating a banana, I looked up to see a man approaching me. He didn't have a dog with him and he wasn't running, so I immediately started to wonder what he was doing at early o'clock on a dark path in the middle of nowhere. Hoping he wasn't a murderer (and that if he was, the smell of my trainers would put him off) I kept my head down and tried to walk past him. By this time the man, and almost certain murderer, was looking directly at me. Then he said, "Hello Claire" and I squinted back through the darkness, surprised that the now-definitely-a-murderer knew who I was. Then I realised it was my good friend Martin Hill, who I hadn't seen for years. He had completed the Half Brutal Triathlon the first year I had organised it, back in 2012. I remembered him because he left his cycling shorts in the marquee and I had returned them after the event. He then started helping out at races, and we became friends.

Martin had a flask of coffee and he poured me a cup as we walked along the side of the canal, chatting about the years since we'd seen each other, catching up on each other's adventures. He had just completed the Spine Race, a very hard, unsupported, 268 mile run along the Pennine Way, held during the winter. I was seriously impressed and congratulated him on his achievement. After a while, we said our goodbyes and he left me for Dartmoor to do some running as I continued to Tiverton.

Most of my thoughts were now focused on finishing. How long would it take me? Would I finish on Tuesday? Could I finish any sooner? I tried to not obsess, but it was hard as all I wanted now was to get off the JOGLE rollercoaster and go home. Over 750 miles in, I was now hitting the hilliest part of the route. While I was struggling down one particularly nasty hill, I noticed my front tyre looked a little worn. On closer inspection, I could see the outer rubber had completely worn away, and the inner layer of canvas was visible through the tyre. This was a first for me as I had never worn through a tyre before, but the almost constant braking (the only brake being on the front wheel) required to control the buggy down the huge hills had pushed the tyre to its limits. Would it last the day, I wondered? I did have a spare, but it was in my kitchen in Dorset. Luckily, my parents were planning on visiting me, so I just needed to ask them to pick it up on their way and I'd be able to change it the following day. I messaged them, then stuck a large piece of Gorilla Tape over the bald spot and hoped for the best.

My day now consisted of going up and down hills. They were relentless. James turned up again, this time with his son Jake, both on their bikes. He handed me some coffee, and more importantly, a couple of hash browns. "Ohmygod" I squealed. "Potato!" They were delicious and I ate them quickly, not realising how hungry I was. I took the opportunity to ask James how far I was from Land's End and how long he thought it would take me.

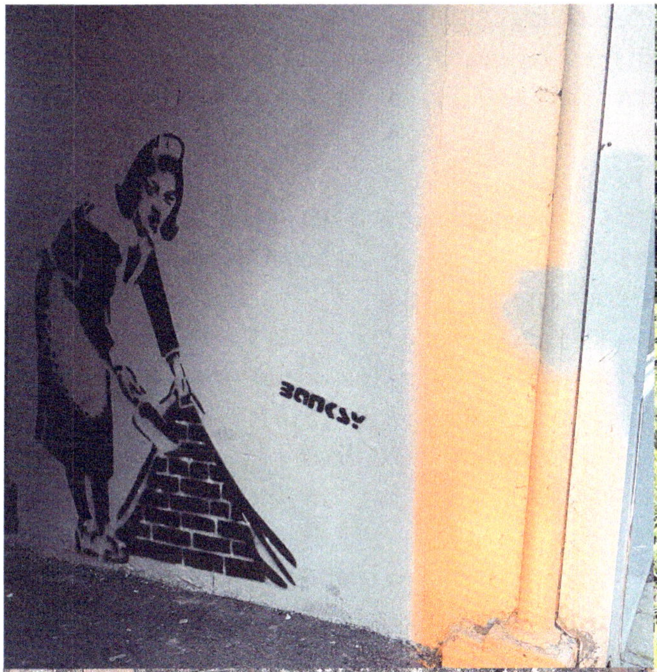
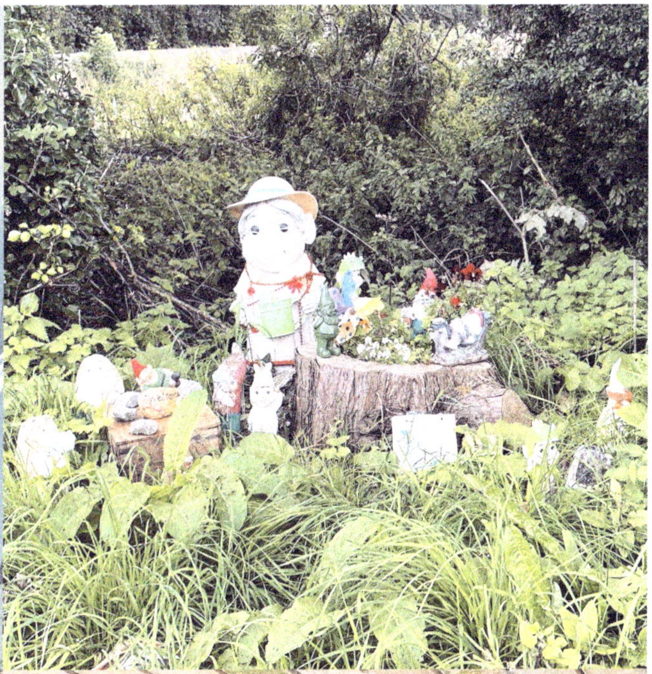
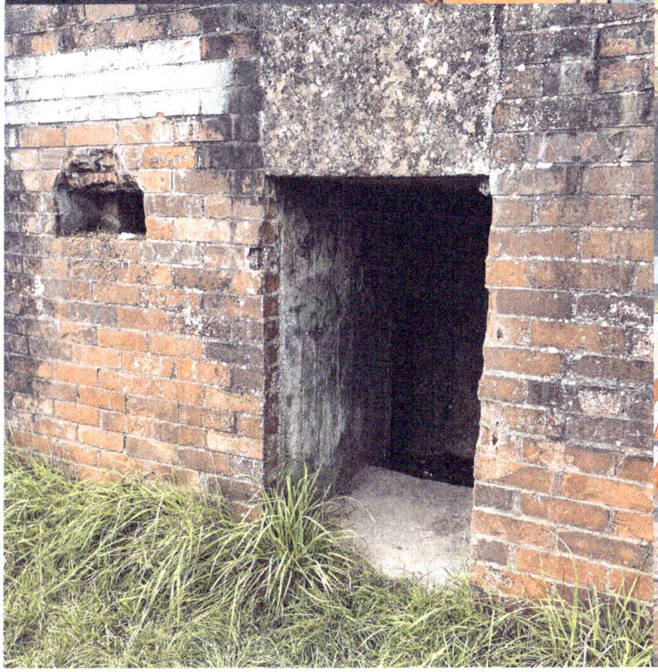
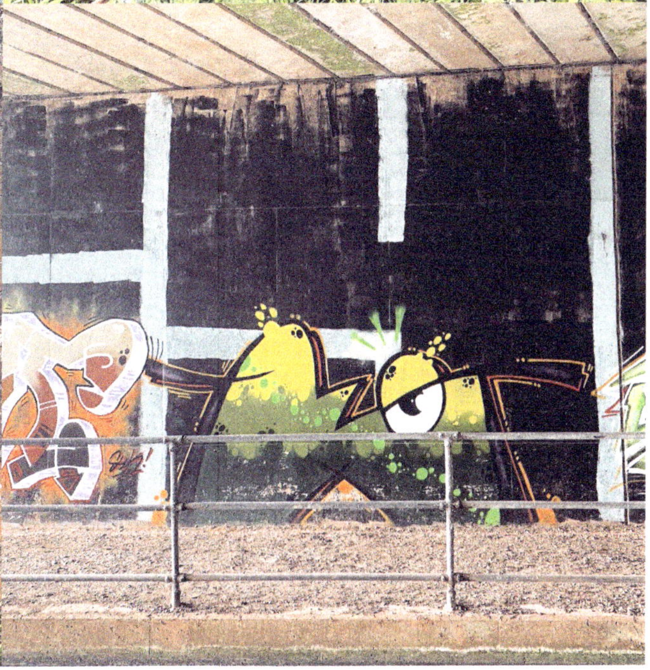

"You are hundreds of miles away," he replied with a grin. "No, seriously…" I whined. "Yes, hundreds," he confirmed, with an evil laugh. James wasn't going to tell me, and from then on would regularly message me to remind me of the hundreds of miles I still had to go, which always made me laugh and also helped keep the remaining distance in perspective.

During the afternoon while I was chatting on the phone to Matthew again (mainly about tyres and how I could repair the front, or swap it with one of the rear ones if needed), I looked up to see a couple of people waiting for me. After a moment or two, I realised it was my best friend Claire and her big brother, Tom. I told Matthew I would chat to him later and ran across the road, grinning from ear to ear. Claire and I had been friends since we were about 14 and had gone to the same girls' school together. We shared the same wicked sense of humour and we had often been told off for giggling away at the back of the classroom. She had been a massive support over the last few weeks, but due to her high-pressured work at the BBC, I didn't think she would be able to actually come and see me on the route.

We had a huge hug, tears rolling down my face. Then I sat on the pavement and chatted away with them both for a good 15 minutes. "How are your poor feet?" asked Claire. I didn't need an excuse to take off my trainers and socks and show them. Tom looked a little green as I proudly pointed out how many toenails I had pulled off, and the large, weeping blisters on the balls of my feet.

Eventually I had to go. It felt wrong leaving Claire, but she promised to come to Bournemouth the following weekend so we could spend some proper time together. It was surreal to think that next week I would be back at home, feeding the cats and putting the washing on. Although it felt weird thinking about it, I really could not wait!

After an hour or so, another Brutal competitor, Sarah Walsh, found me. She had won the JurassicMan Extreme Triathlon a few years ago and I remembered her for the finish line cartwheel she had performed, impressing us all. Sarah was great company. We chatted about all things racing and after we ran out of triathlon talk, we moved on to life in general. Chatting with Sarah was a great distraction for me, taking my mind off the pain that was building in my feet as I got close to the end of the day.

Tonight, I was treating myself to a Travel Lodge and I was excited about the prospect of a decent night's sleep as the last two had been so awful. After 44 miles, I finally made it into my hotel room. I quickly sorted out my kit, put everything on charge and finally relaxed in a hot bath, drinking some chocolate milkshake that Martin had given me earlier that morning. Afterwards, I sat on the bed and inspected my feet. Today I had noticed that my left toes had been hitting the front of my shoe, but looking at my foot now, I couldn't see that it was swollen in any way. Apart from the massive blisters, it looked normal. I mentioned my concerns in the basecamp group and Gavin said that he'd had the same experience when his arches collapsed. "I went up a half size," he confirmed. "Wow," I said to myself, weirdly impressed that I may have developed an injury during this challenge that I had never experienced before.

As I snuggled down into the huge duvet, I allowed myself to think about the remaining time I had left. I had two big days of 40-ish miles, and then hopefully a cheeky marathon to finish up at Land's End on Tuesday. The end was finally in sight.

Day 22: Sunday 6th September

Okehampton to Bodmin - 38.28 miles - **Total mileage: 826.9**

This morning involved a lot of procrastinating. Making yet another cup of coffee before leaving the hotel, then faffing repeatedly with my kit. I was at the point in the challenge where I had nearly finished, but with 100 miles still to go, the JOGLE was not quite done with me yet. I was in a weird no man's land, where I was still in the routine of covering 40 miles a day, finding food, somewhere to sleep and dealing with all the normal issues, but my head had gone home and was sat patiently waiting on the sofa for my body to join it.

I finally got out the door at 6:00am and spent the first part of the morning on a lovely bike path which I shared with a couple of runners and dog walkers. After that, it was a blur of lanes and country roads where everyone drove just a little too fast. However, I had reached a point where I didn't care anymore. Huge lorries steamed past me and I barely reacted. I wasn't sure if this was a good thing or not.

Another puncture. As I stopped to change the inner tube, hoping it would be for the last time, my mum messaged to say they were on their way. I was glad, as both the buggy and I needed some support. The buggy needed a new front tyre because it was almost completely worn through. It was raining again, so I couldn't even bodge a repair with tape. I just needed a hug, as my morale was low. My left foot had split on the slide and for such a tiny cut it was disproportionally painful.

For most of the morning it rained on and off, with some really heavy showers where I'd have to change in and out of my waterproofs several times. As I reached the Cornish border just before midday, the sun came out and I took some 'Welcome to Cornwall' photos for Instagram. It dawned on me that this was the final county border I would cross, and I really was going to finish this.

My parents showed up and after hugs all round, Alan pulled a new tyre from the back of the car and I took the

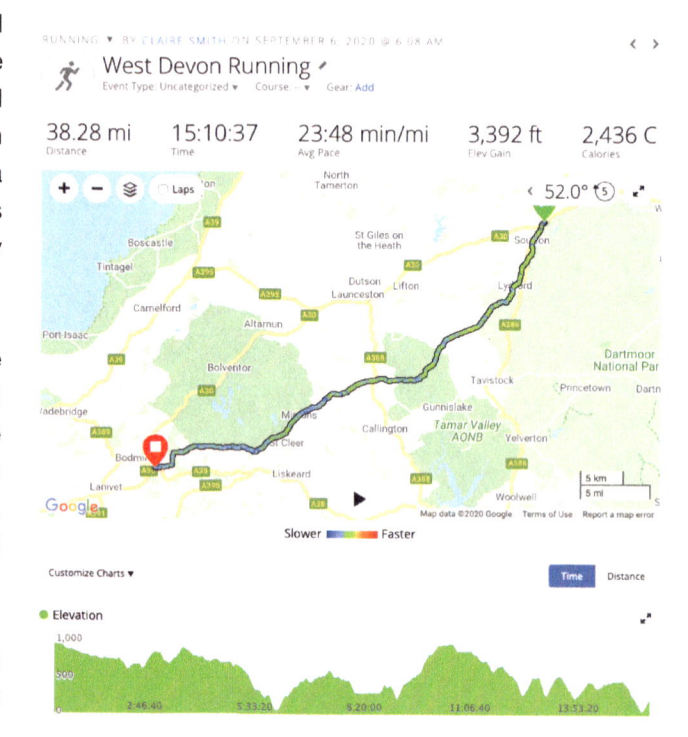

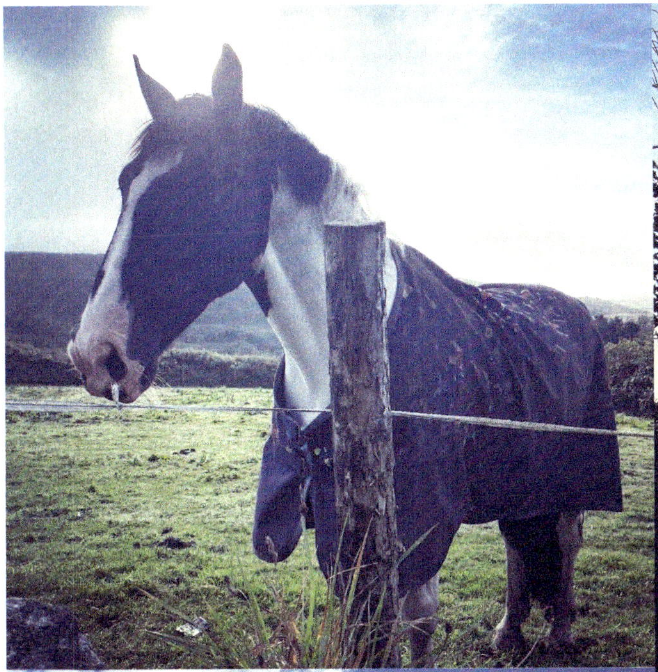
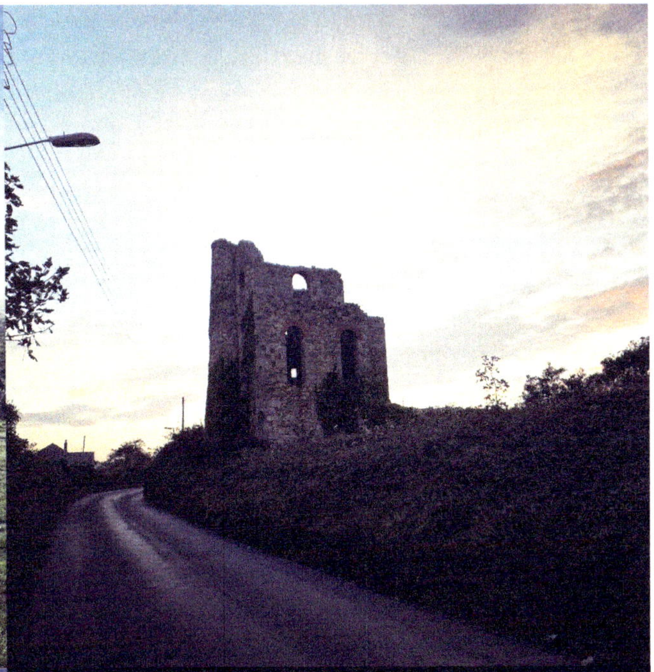
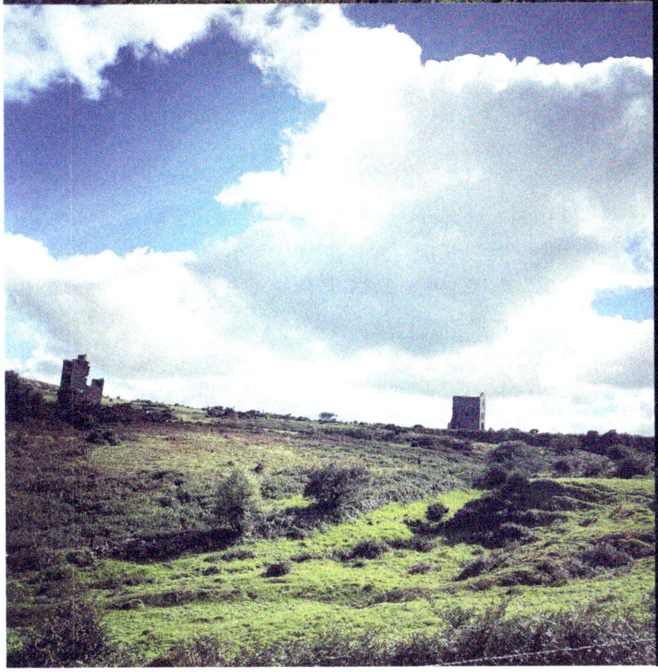
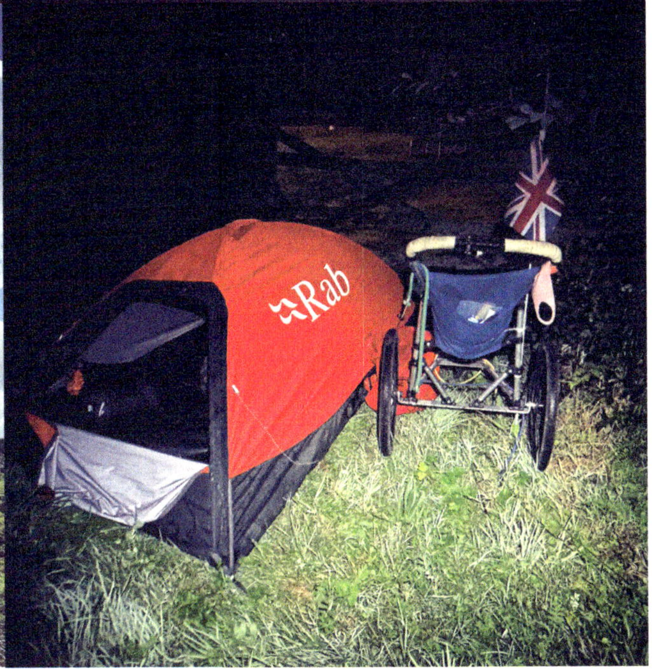
Rab

old one off the buggy. It definitely wouldn't have survived many more miles with these hills. My mum was keen for me to find another hotel for the night, but I explained that I had looked and there really wasn't anything suitable in the area that I could likely reach that day. She looked concerned but I shrugged and said, "I'm fine with camping, I like it". In reality I was actually pretty sick of it; not so much sleeping in the tent, but finding a good, safe place to pitch up. Wild camping was not fun anymore.

Later that afternoon I passed through a village called Minions. This amused me no end as I took another road sign photo for social media. Surrounded with lush green views and some engine house ruins, it even had a cool stone circle. The sheep were quite pretty, too. Although I complemented them on their looks, they seemed unimpressed, continuing to eat grass and barely acknowledging my presence.

The afternoon was the closest thing I could get to a rollercoaster without actually being on a rollercoaster. Pushing the buggy up ridiculously steep lanes, then hanging on for dear life as it pulled me down the other side. Over and over again, hammering my legs and feet, my progress painful slow. I cursed Cornwall for its unrelenting undulations and yearned for flat roads again.

As the sun got lower in the sky, I looked at Google maps to see where I was headed and check for somewhere to camp. It didn't look good. At my current location, both sides of the road were thickly wooded with nowhere flat in sight. After that I would be heading into Bodmin, which was obviously a built-up area and again unsuitable for pitching a tent. I pushed on feeling anxious that I wouldn't be able to find anywhere to sleep. After all the hills, I was exhausted.

I turned left onto a small and very quiet lane. It was now pitch dark and I could just make out a few large houses but not much else. I came to a gateway and reluctantly decided that it would have to do. Although it was on the side of the road, it was also the garden entrance of one of the large properties. I hoped that the owners wouldn't notice me. Once the tent was up and I had sorted out my kit, I got into both sleeping bags. It was cold and I felt rough. I couldn't be bothered to boil any water for food and I also felt uneasy about where I was camped. Another restless night followed. I couldn't get comfortable in the tent and shivered despite my many layers. As I lay there, trying and failing to fall asleep, I sincerely hoped this would be my last night under canvas.

Day 23: Monday 7th September

Bodmin to Camborne - 41.4 miles - **Total mileage: 868.3**

At 3:00am I finally gave up on sleep. I struggled out of my sleeping bags and started to quickly pack down the tent as quietly as I could. Then, just as I was fixing the dry bags to the buggy, a dog started to bark loudly. I looked towards the house and saw a light come on. "Shit" I muttered, pulling the bungy cords around my kit. The next thing I heard was the sound of a door opening, a woman's voice, and then a massive dog running over to the gate. I hastily decided my bags were secure enough, switched off my head torch and started running down the road, adrenaline pumping. I hadn't been trespassing exactly, but it kind of felt like I had.

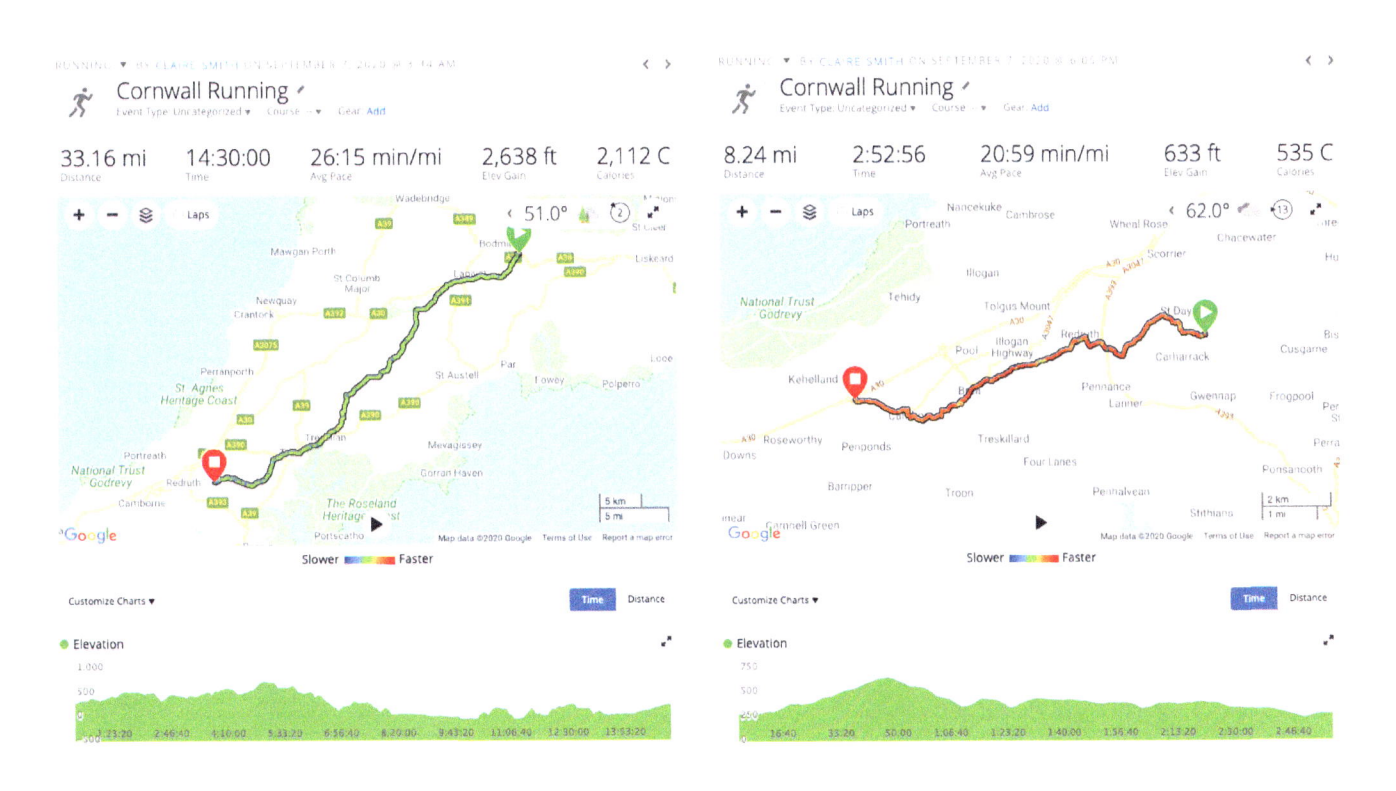

No sleep or proper food and a bad start to the day had me feeling low. I shook my head and said to myself "I'm going to finish this tomorrow; I really need to cheer up a bit." I scrabbled around for some snacks and tried to pick up the pace a bit. Once I was through Bodmin and back on country roads, I discovered that my head torch was about to die. After a fruitless search for spare batteries, I realised that I had used them all and cursed myself for not buying more yesterday. It was still only 4:00am and I had hours of darkness left.

Just as I was trying to work out what to do, I looked up and to my absolute horror realised that something very large and very fast was headed straight for me. I hurled myself and the buggy into the bushes and braced myself. The lorry driver did not see me at all and just hurtled past. For the second time that morning I felt a huge rush of adrenaline, realising how close that had been. I was on the right side of the road facing the traffic, but due to the darkness couldn't see that the road also curved around to the right. The bend made it impossible for the lorry driver to see me, or me him.

I took a deep breath and tried to get my heart rate back down. Then I remembered my phone torch, and that I had a full battery pack to recharge it later. I pulled my phone from its normal place on top of my dry bag and flicked on the light. It was bright enough for me to see the road and more importantly, other road users could now see me. Still feeling shaky after my brush with death, I found some chocolate and a couple of biscuits in my bag, which I ate for a blood sugar boost. After a while I felt better, and even saw the funny (if not slightly dark) side of almost being killed the day before finishing the JOGLE.

The never-ending hills continued throughout the morning and the roads got busier and busier. Just before midday Kathi arrived, which lifted my spirits immensely. She handed me a few packets of crisps and some Wagon Wheels, which I hadn't had in years. Munching on the biscuits, we laughed about me almost being hit by lorries and cars. I needed to have a good laugh about it, because otherwise I probably would have cried.

After Kathi went off to find her campsite, my parents turned up again. My mum told me I looked tired, which made me laugh out loud. "Mum, of course I look tired, I've just run here from Scotland." She looked confused for a moment and then said "Well, you looked better yesterday." I told her about my eventful morning, and she shook her head. "I'll be glad when you've finished this, it's not good for my nerves". I knew exactly what she meant; it wasn't doing my nerves much good either.

Once I was on my own again, I found myself back on quiet country lanes. A few more hills later, my feet were really starting to complain. "We're only halfway through the day" I said to them, "so there's no point getting all angry when we still have bloody hours to go. Just pipe down!" Unsurprisingly this little pep talk made no difference whatsoever, so whilst I was passing through a small village, I decided to have a rest at a bus stop.

When I was a kid, bus stops used to have proper seats. But during my JOGLE I had noticed that every single one now had a weird partial-bench, where you could half lean, half sit. This was probably enough if you were just waiting ten minutes for the bus, but if you were completely shattered with bleeding feet, they were rubbish! Anyway, there wasn't any alternative and I needed to stop for a minute, so I perched on the seat, took my trainers off and rubbed my feet. The combination of pain, ecstasy and exhaustion was too much, and I burst into tears. I rested my head on the handlebars of the buggy and whilst massaging my feet, I just cried and cried. After about five minutes I put my shoes back on, wiped my face and started to run again.

I made my way through Truro and phoned Matthew for a team talk to distract me from the day I was having. I told him about blubbing at the bus stop, to which he said, "Crying is fine, as long as you keep moving."

"But it's too far!" I whined. "No it isn't," came the reply straight back. "You'll be finished in three hours. How far have you got left tomorrow?"

I told him it was 24 miles to Land's End. *"24 miles?! Is that it!?!"* Matthew then reminded me that during the Mexico Double Deca I'd completed the previous year, I swam 48 miles, cycled 2240 miles, then ran 524 miles to finish in third place, even though I thought my foot was going to fall off half way through. He reminded me of my struggles with alcohol, body image, depression, and that I had beaten them all. He listed other challenges I had overcome in the past and said that I would get through this too, one step at a time. He ended with "Suck it up Smith, you're nearly there. Give me a call when you get to the finish."

Once I'd made it through Truro, I was back on lanes again and climbing yet more hills. I was really struggling now; I just couldn't understand how the day before the finish had become one of the hardest of the whole challenge. My feet screamed, so I relented and sat on the ground next to the road. Laying down, I put my feet up on the buggy and gasped with relief as the pain drained out of them. For a moment, the world became fuzzy and I must have dropped off to sleep. "Are you okay?" a voice said. I stirred and looked up to find a car next to me with a lady leaning out of the passenger window, a concerned look on her face. "Oh yeah, I'm fine" I said. "Thanks for asking though" I added, touched that she had stopped.

I hauled myself off the ground and forced myself on. I had a hotel booked for tonight and I was going to finish tomorrow, why wasn't I happy? I should be over the moon and this day should be brilliant, but it was endless and awful. I turned a corner and a huge "Road Closed" sign faced me. There were a lot of workers in Hi-Viz jackets milling about, resurfacing the road. I looked at the diversion on my navigation app and almost had a seizure. It was miles longer than my planned route. The thought of adding so much as a few hundred metres by this point would be enough to finish me off.

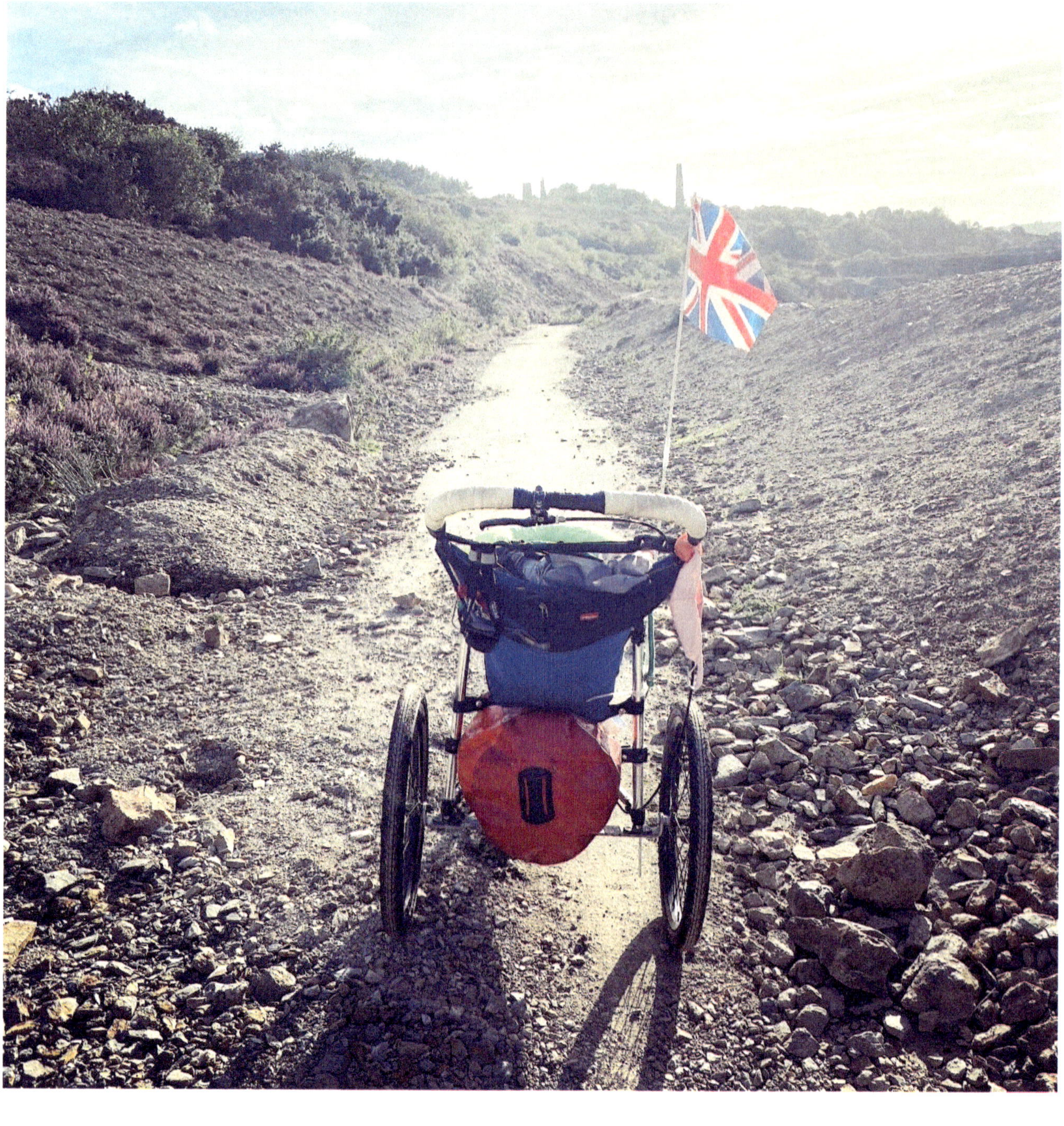

I approached one of the workmen. Trying not to burst into tears, I attempted to explain my situation and ask/beg if I could use the road, even though it was closed. The man looked a little confused, as most people did when I explained what I was doing, but then to my utter relief he said "Yeah, go on then love." I almost hugged him but managed to control myself. I settled on thanking him about five times, then quickly walked off before anyone could stop me. All the other workers looked on, bemused and open mouthed.

At mile 31 I followed the route onto another bike path. This one was really rocky and a little difficult to push the buggy over. I began to get the normal anxious feelings about the jogger breaking, but then realised I was so close to the end that if it did happen I could just ditch a load of stuff and carry the bare minimum. This was a good, although slightly surreal, feeling. But it made me realise that my buggy and I had started this together, and I wanted us both to finish it, too. I mentally willed the jogger not to break. "We only have another 24 hours to get through" I said to it.

Once I was back on the road, I found that yet more stupidly big hills lay in wait for me. "Head down and suck it up, Smith," I reminded myself of Matthew's advice from earlier that day. I put in my earphones and lost myself in music for the next few hours. As I got closer to Camborne, where my parents were going to meet me for a mile or two, the realisation that this was the last evening I would spend on the road hit me. My eyes filled with tears for what seemed like the hundredth time that day, but this time they were happy tears. From what started as a crazy idea just a few months ago, I had somehow managed to make it down the full length of the UK and raise a decent amount of money in the process. Not bad for someone who is rubbish at running and has no sense of direction, I thought, smiling to myself.

Camborne followed Redruth, and as promised, my mum and Alan were waiting for me a few miles from the hotel. We walked past engine room ruins which looked amazing in the sunset, then into the town which, despite being late, was still very busy. It seemed to take forever to reach the Premier Inn and I felt myself getting annoyed at everything and everyone as I was so low and depleted. It had been an extremely tough day and I just wanted it to be over. Once I had checked in and said good night to my folks, I went to my room and sat on the bed. Kicking off my trainers and pulling off my socks, I lay back and closed my eyes.

It was almost over.

Day 24: Tuesday 8th September
Camborne to Land's End - 24.62 miles - **Total mileage: 892.92**

I woke up early, excited as a kid on Christmas morning. Today I had a mere 24 miles to go and I would have run, walked, hobbled, and at times almost crawled, the entire length of the UK. But right now, the only thing I cared about was stopping.

I sorted my kit and packed the jogger for the last time. As I pulled on my clothes, I hoped I didn't smell too much. I had basically worn the same two tops for the whole challenge but they seemed okay, to me at least. My trainers were a different story though and smelt absolutely disgusting. Once I had sorted all my kit and was ready to go, I quietly closed the hotel door behind me and made my way to reception.

It was dark outside and the roads were blissfully quiet. Looking at the map on my navigation app, it still didn't seem real that just over three weeks ago I had started on that dark, chilly morning in Scotland; alone, with the wind whipping around me as I fiddled with my kit and the tracker. Ultra-distance challenges often feel like they're never going to end, so it's sometimes hard to believe it when they do. Now here I was, on the final stretch.

After four miles I came to a large petrol station. Switching off my head torch, I went inside and bought some breakfast and other snacks for later that morning. I also got a large coffee as I was definitely still half asleep. But my mood was up, and I had to stop myself from telling random people that today I was finishing the JOGLE. I reminded myself that to everybody else, today was just a normal Tuesday and they were off to work or doing other mundane activities.

As the sun rose behind me, I could see the lights of Penzance in the distance. I hoped today wouldn't be too hilly, but I had cycled this part before so knew it wasn't going to be flat. Still, after the last few days of this journey I could cope with anything. The morning went by quickly. A few people beeped their horns in support as they passed me, and a nice couple from Brutal came and said hello and well done. Kathi arrived and we hugged and chatted excitedly about the finish.

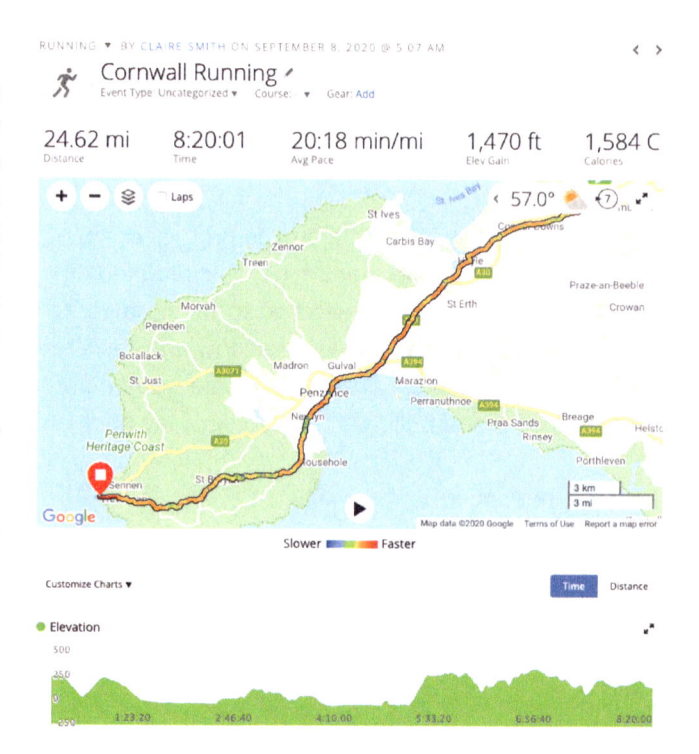

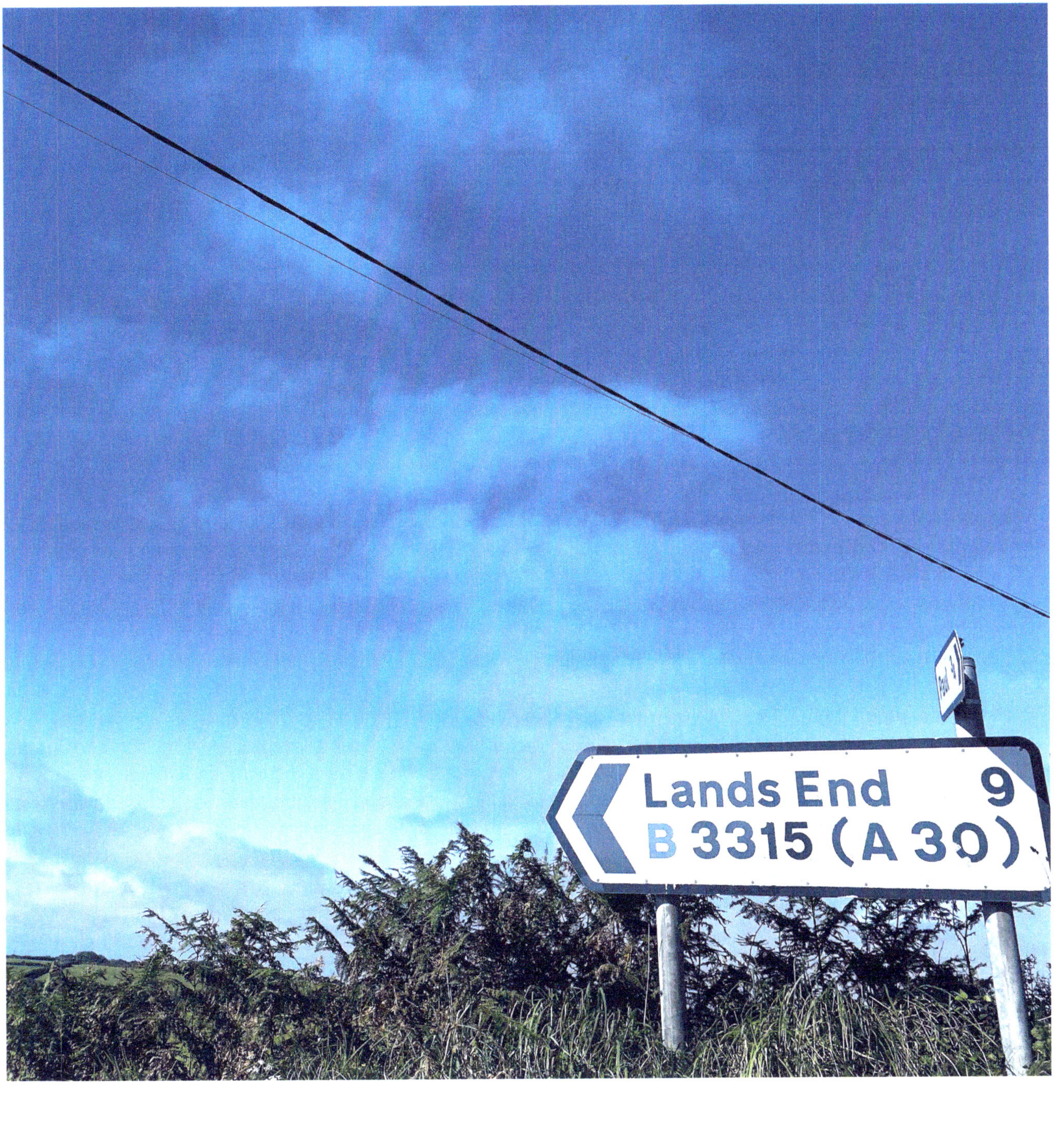
Lands End 9
B 3315 (A 30)

She and Gavin had been such an integral part of the challenge - without them it would have been so much harder, and definitely a lot duller. Their animated conversations in the basecamp messenger group often made me laugh out loud. But more importantly for me, I always felt that they had been there, and that even if I was in the middle of nowhere at night, I could message and one or both would answer me. Yes, this had been a self-supported journey, but I had never felt alone on it.

More roads, more miles. I started to feel impatient, wanting to be at Land's End already, but I still had a long way to go, especially on broken and bleeding feet. Once I arrived in Penzance, I made my way along the seafront. It was a beautiful day, the sun was shining and made the sea sparkle. A lady stopped to ask me what I was doing, and I explained that I had ran here from Scotland. Normally, I was really happy to chat to strangers, in fact it had become something I really enjoyed, but today I just wanted to keep moving. The woman seemed to pick up on this and said "I'll let you get on then, but well done" I thanked her and went on my way. A little further down the road I was stopped again, this time by an older man. "Are you running a marathon?" he asked me, laughing. I looked at him and tried to reply, but I was in such a rush the words must have come out like "AbitmorethanamarathonI'vejustranfromJohno'GroatsandI'mgoingto Land'sEndbutI'magainsttheclocksoI'vegottogo,bye!" As I ran off down the road, I could tell from the confused look on his face that I'd left him none the wiser, but I didn't have time to stop and explain.

To get out of Penzance I had to climb a large hill. I had seen it on my navigation app, and I knew it was going to be a tough one. The elevation line on the diagram looked almost vertical. To make matters worse, it was a narrow lane with cars parked on either side. Vehicles were driving up and down, weaving in and out of spaces and the pavement was extremely narrow, impossible for me and the jogger to fit on to. I looked up the huge hill and just thought, "Fuck it. The cars will have to deal with me being on the road today." I'd had enough of trying to be considerate. Just this once, they could wait for me.

By the time I reached the top I was out of breath and sweating, but at least it hadn't taken too long. Now on lanes again, I had just nine miles to go. On a normal JOGLE day that wouldn't even be a quarter of my target mileage, but today nine miles felt overwhelmingly far. I switched on my music to take my mind off the distance, but it didn't work. I tried an audiobook, but I wasn't really listening to it. I just obsessed over the miles, counting down. Nine, eight, seven… come on! I willed them to go faster. I just wanted to get to the finish.

With about four miles to go, a couple of cyclists joined me for a while. We chatted over how hard UK roads can be, and what a shame it is that a lot of motorists are so inconsiderate to other road users. One of the riders, Rich, had a camera on his bike specifically for recording bad drivers. After a while, they said goodbye and that they'd see me at the finish.

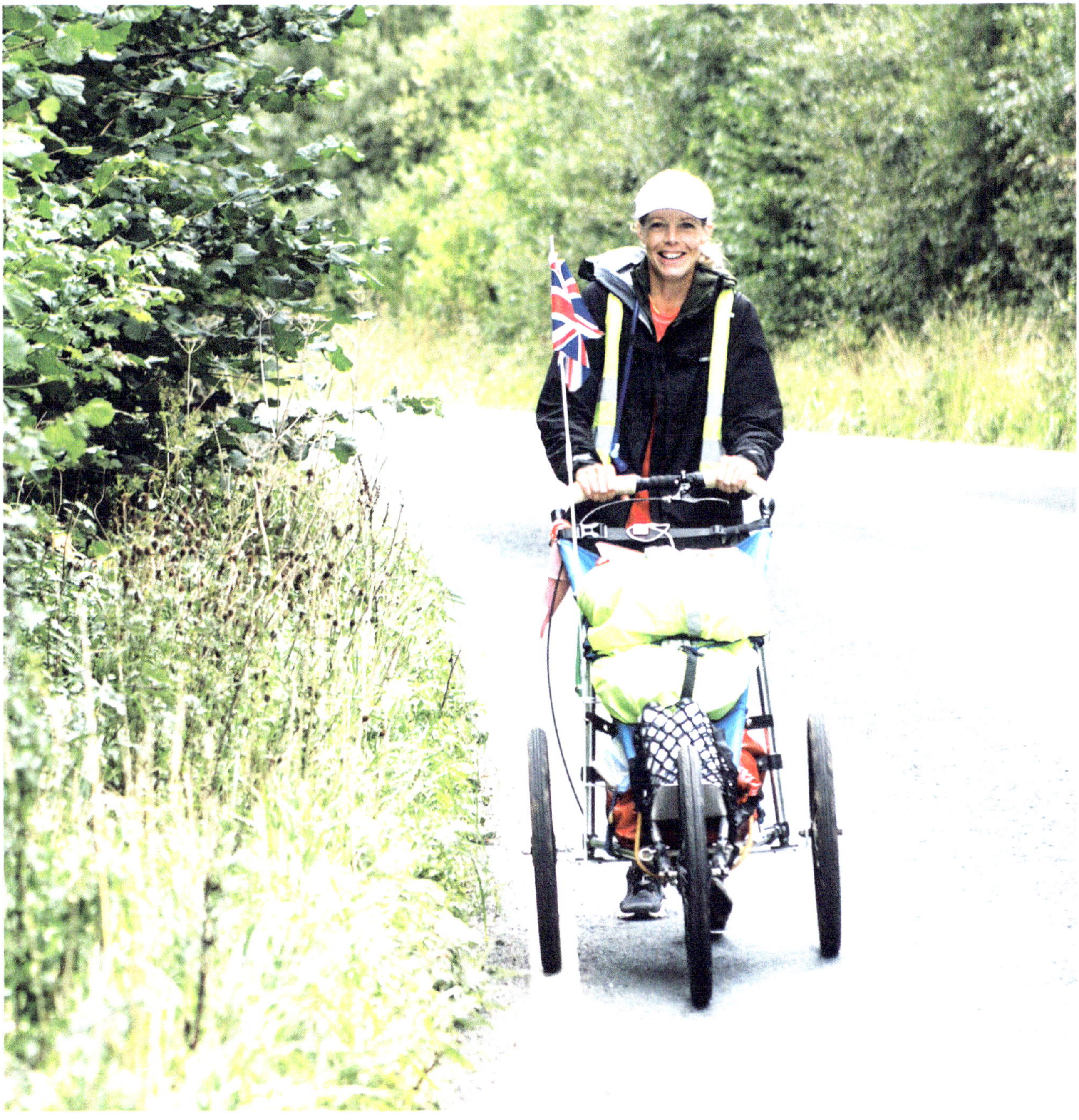

As I got through the final village, I noticed that I only had one mile to go. Adrenaline surged through me and I started to run. At first my body complained at the dramatic change of pace, but it soon settled in and I began to enjoy it. As I ran, I thought that I would be feeling more emotional but all I felt was impatience. Maybe after all the tears yesterday I didn't have any left.

Finally, the entrance gates of Land's End visitor centre lay ahead of me. There was a large queue of traffic leading up to them so I stopped in line, wondering what I should do next. I hadn't really thought about it being so busy, but the car park attendant saw me and waved me onwards. I quickly ran down the centre of the cars, hoping that nobody opened their doors on me. I could hear some people cheering for me and I looked up to see Debbie, a friend who had completed the Brutal Oner Ultra Run the year before. She and a few others were standing on a mound of grass, clapping and shouting. I grinned and waved at them, feeling a little overwhelmed.

As I ran through the gates and towards the famous Land's End sign, everybody started to clap and cheer. People who didn't even know what I was doing were applauding. It was a wonderful and yet slightly surreal moment. I kept running and finally saw the white signpost, which to my horror was surrounded by people. A large queue snaked down the path of folk wanting their picture taken with it. Once again, I hadn't planned for this scenario. I had always imagined it would be late at night when I finished, with only a few people around. But instead it was a warm, sunny day and the place was heaving with holiday makers. Kathi, thankfully, had planned for it being busy and she had cleared it with the kiosk staff so that when I turned up, I could basically jump the queue.

Feeling a little guilty and apologising to the people who had been waiting patiently for their photos, the buggy and I stood by the sign whilst Kathi and the official Land's End photographer snapped away. This was it, I thought. I'd actually done it. It had taken me 23 days, 8 hours, and a fair few more miles than I'd originally planned, but I'd finished. Still there were no tears, I just felt happy and relieved.

After the photos had been taken, I found my mum and gave her a big hug. She told me how proud she was of me, and how well I'd done with the fundraising. Over £6,000 had been donated to the Forest Holme Hospice, which was way beyond my expectations. A few more hugs and congratulations from everybody, then we started walking back towards the car park. "Do you want anything to eat?" my mum asked me, always trying to feed me up. I did, but I wasn't sure what. Then I looked up and saw we were outside an ice cream shop. I gestured towards it and said, "That's exactly what I need right now".

So Kathi, my folks and me, all sat on a wall enjoying our ice creams in the sun. The jogger was next to me, like a faithful old dog. I couldn't help but feel a little sad that our adventure had come to an end. But my main emotion was one of relief.

We had done it.

LAND'S END
2020
NEW YORK 3147
JOHN O'GROATS 874
ISLES OF SCILLY 28
LONGSHIPS LIGHTHOUSE 1½
BRUTAL JOGLE
8TH SEPTEMBER

Epilogue

Along with my sleeping bag and tent, I left the buggy in the back of my parent's car when we got back to the hotel. Feeling weirdly guilty I went up to my room for the first time on this journey without it. Once I was in my room, I enjoyed a few hours of pure relaxation, something that I'd not been able to do for the last 23 days. I didn't have to charge anything or dry any kit. I didn't need to dress my feet and hunt for clean socks. No need to refill water bottles or my CamelBak ready for tomorrow. Finally, I could just chill.

I made a cup of tea, had a long hot soak in the bath and enjoyed the fact that I didn't have to get up at 4:00am the next day. Once I was dressed in some clean clothes that my daughter had sent via my mum, I looked at my trainers in the corner of the room. They had done me proud, but their time was up. I dumped them in the bin, feeling bad for the cleaners who would find them the following day.

An hour or so later I met my folks in reception, and we went out for some decent food. After a large plate of lasagne and chips followed by waffles with ice cream, I started slipping into an exhausted coma. I genuinely don't remember walking back to my hotel room and getting into bed, just waking up at dawn and realising that I didn't have to get up - then going back to sleep again with a smile on my face.

The next day we returned home. I stood in my living room surrounded by bags and equipment, feeling like I'd been gone much longer than three weeks. The house was empty, as my daughter was on holiday and my son was now living in university accommodation. The cats were all in though, and gave me the normal post-event welcome. Samuel wanted attention, Bailey wanted feeding, and Dexter wanted me to leave him alone.

I unpacked my kit and set the washing machine to the special setting for really disgusting, dirty clothes. After everything was done, I made a cup of tea and collapsed on the sofa. Exhaustion overwhelmed me. Just standing up for a few minutes was too much right now. It's funny how you can keep going to the finish of ultra-events, but as soon as you stop, your body shuts down.

The next few days were spent doing basically the same. I would get up and unload the dishwasher, then need to sit down for a bit. Put some more washing on, and then have to take a break. I felt like a 90-year old. Eating was hard too. I needed small portions at regular intervals, and my blood sugar would suddenly drop without warning, leaving me weak and wobbly.

Sleeping involved constantly dreaming that I was still in the middle of the JOGLE, waking up sweating and wondering where I was, and then having to tell myself (again) that I had actually managed to finish it and I could go back to sleep.

My feet took the longest to get back to normal. They were a real state by the finish, with only a couple of toenails left, chunks of skin missing and other bits peeling off. They were also bright red like they had been burnt and if I stood for too long, they throbbed. Both of my second toes were numb and tingly for a month after. When I eventually started running again, the temperature had dropped, and the soles of my feet felt numb from all the nerve damage. Something I'd experienced the year before after completing the Mexican Double Deca.

But everything eventually heals, and life returns to normal. I got back to training about three weeks after finishing the JOGLE. Apart from a sore hamstring (which was sore before I even left for Scotland but was definitely worse afterwards), everything felt good. Running without a buggy was a little weird though… A few people asked me if I had post-event blues and although I felt like I should have, I've never really suffered from it. Once I finish something, I'm always looking to the next challenge, the next adventure, and I try not to look back too much. I like to live my life without regrets. I don't want to come to the end of it thinking, "I wish I'd done that."

…And I did get that FKT!

Lessons Learnt

What would I do differently if I did the JOGLE again? (I'm definitely not doing it again. EVER.) The following is a list of lessons from the JOGLE, ultra-distance racing, and life in general.

Train with the kit you are going to use. Obviously, it would have been good to have sorted out how I was going to carry my kit earlier on, and then I could have trained with the buggy more. Some off-road, trail sections and hill preparation would have been good, as going downhill with the jogger was very hard - something I had not anticipated.

More detailed route planning. I honestly thought I would be able to use the same route that Dan Lawson and Carla Moninaro had run a few weeks before I made my attempt. But the reality was that with a buggy, I was much slower and wider than these amazing record-breaking athletes. I also struggled without support crew on bikes or vans, helping me with traffic management. It wouldn't be *impossible* to run the record route with a baby jogger, but there were times that I genuinely felt my life was at risk with the vast amounts traffic on the fast, narrow roads. In the end, I'm glad I made the decision to add some extra miles by using safer roads.

Eat and drink more and take my iron supplements. I've always struggled with anaemia and I went into the challenge at below the recommended Ferritin level, so it was no surprise that it was even lower when I'd finished. I was definitely feeling weaker and had more dizzy spells in the last five days.

Spares. I could have taken an extra tyre and spares for 'exotic' parts like the jogger axels, which would have been very hard to find en route. Although I managed to sort these issues out, they could have taken me a lot longer had I not been so lucky. Having said that, it's all part of the adventure with these sorts of challenges and you can't plan for everything. If you did, you would never leave home.

Other than that, everything worked well. I truly believe that you can plan the life out of adventures sometimes. Getting out there and having to deal with problems on the go is what it's all about. I really enjoy the challenge of facing the unknown and having to deal with things that I'm not expecting.

Blood tests / weight loss

My post-JOGLE blood test results were pretty much as expected. My ferritin levels were lower than pre-JOGLE, which was not surprising. Obviously, the physical stress of running the length of the UK combined with a sometimes less-than-optimal garage forecourt diet contributed to the lower readings, but during the event I was also not as disciplined as I should have been with taking iron supplements. During the final week I starting to experience dizzy spells which were indicative of iron deficiency, and this was born out in my B12 and folate markers. Other blood markers of iron metabolism and storage such as transferrin saturation were in keeping with iron deficiency (something I have struggled with for a number of years).

Also unsurprisingly, there was a drop in my cholesterol levels between the pre and post-JOGLE tests (if my cholesterol had gone *up* after running almost 900 miles, I don't know what I would do!) My renal panel showed fluctuation in clearance of the kidneys which was indicative of dehydration. Again, drinking enough liquid on events is a constant struggle for me as I rarely feel thirsty, so this was entirely in keeping with what would be expected.

I was very pleased to see that my liver enzymes were all within normal limits post-JOGLE and had not changed significantly from the pre-event values. Endurance athletes can experience raised bilirubin levels (a marker of liver function as well as red blood cell breakdown) due to foot-strike haemolysis (as the name suggests, a type of anaemia seen in long-distance runners, resulting from damage caused by impact with road/pavement), but despite the shocking appearance of my feet at the finish, I didn't experience this condition.

For the past 15 years I have been operating with only half a thyroid, so even though my Thyroid Stimulating Hormone results were borderline low for normal reference ranges, I was still pretty happy with the result. A slight drop between pre/post-JOGLE values, but nothing significant. I was also glad to see that my COVID-19 antibodies remained negative in the post-JOGLE test.

The most obvious physiological change I experienced was weight loss, but it went back on easily enough during my recovery (mainly through eating copious amounts of Maltesers).

Before weight - 124lbs

After weight - 110lbs

Food and nutrition

Eating during very long, hard endurance challenges can be difficult. You may not be able to eat enough to replace the energy you expend, at which point weight loss becomes inevitable (I lost 14lb during the JOGLE). You may also experience stomach issues and sickness.

In my experience of fuelling for events, the more normal the food, the better. It's also worth being flexible, as unless you are in a very controlled environment you will need to eat what you can find or are given. If you are in a foreign country it can be even more challenging, so plan ahead.

During the JOGLE I ate a lot of pork pies, sandwiches, wraps and fruit. At the end of the day I would boil water and cook a dehydrated Firepot meal or a Pot Noodle. A hot meal makes a big difference to your morale.

I used one Precision Hydration tablet per day to help with dehydration and electrolyte loss. However, as the weather was mostly cloudy and raining, over-heating wasn't a massive issue on this event (unlike previous races in Mexico and Switzerland).

I also ate 1 - 2 sachets of Resilient Nutrition (nut butter) a day. I found these particularly good mid-morning, as they would keep me going until I found a shop to restock. They also didn't give me spikes/crashes with my blood sugar levels as some snack foods do, like cereal bars or chocolate.

My appetite changed over the three weeks or so. During the first few days I struggled to eat, but as the time went on it got easier. In the middle section, I was constantly starving and after enduring Storm Francis on day 10 I went to a Burger King and ordered a cheeseburger, fries, onion rings and a vanilla milk shake. Even though it was junk food, it was one the best meals I'd had in ages. Towards the end of the JOGLE, I began to lose my appetite again. I'd lost a lot of weight by then and knew how important it was to keep my strength up, but I still found it difficult to eat.

It's a good idea to make a nutrition plan for these type of challenges and ensure that you train with the foods you are likely to consume beforehand, but also be able to change the plan if need be. I would also advise putting on a bit of weight if you have a low body fat percentage to start with.

RESILIENT NUTRITION
LONG RANGE FUEL
WAITROSE & PARTNERS
CHANA MASALA & SPINACH
WITH COCONUT MAYO
25 AUG
JETBOIL
JETBOIL
IREPOT
CHILLI CON CARNE
GREGGS

Kit list

Clothing
- Buff
- Hi-Viz jacket
- Waterproof jacket
- Lightweight jacket
- Waterproof trousers
- Compression calf guards
- Waterproof gloves
- Pants x4
- Socks x4
- Spare leggings
- Spare long-sleeved top
- Spare short-sleeved top
- DHB visor
- Warm zip up hoody
- Flip flops
- Spare trainers
- Sunglasses

Sleep
- Sleeping bag
- Roll mat
- Tent

Food
- Hydration tablets (Precision Hydration)
- X10 Sachets of Resilient Nutrition
- Coffee sachets
- Travel mug
- Spork x2
- De-hydrated food x4 (Firepot)
- JetBoil
- Gas canister
- Lighter x2

Electrical
- Battery packs x6
- Cables and charges
- Head Torch x2
- X2 Garmin watches
- X2 Garmin Edges (didn't use these)
- Batteries

Mechanical / bike
- Gorilla tape
- X3 spare inner tubes (bought 8 more on route)
- Pump (wrong one, had to buy a new one!)
- Tyre levers and other tools
- Puncture repair kit (never used)
- Bike lock

Medical / self-care
- Wipes
- Physio tape
- Medicated talc
- Vaseline
- Mosquito spray and net
- Sun cream (rarely used)
- Toothbrush and paste
- Small towel
- Medical pack (inc. Compeed, tape and painkillers)

Random
- 2 safety pins (blisters!)
- Laminated route maps (these got binned very quickly!)
- Sponsorship / tracker link cards (to give out)
- A Glow Bug *(a glow-in-the-dark toy I had from when I was 10 that my mum forced me to take for good luck!)*
- Waterproof case for phone (used a lot!)
- CamelBak and bag
- Cable ties
- Bum bag (for Jogger handles)
- Money

All the small items of my kit were placed in organised, clear zip lock bags, i.e. Batteries and head torches in one bag. Physio tape, pain killers and plasters in another. This made it easier to grab what I needed. Otherwise it would have been like putting my hand into a lucky dip every time I opened the dry bag.

Drop Box Contents
(packs I posted to 3 locations en route)
- Gas canister
- X4 Dehydrated meals (Firepot)
- X10 Sachets of Resilient Nutrition
- Hydration tablets (Precision Hydration)
- Compeed
- Painkillers
- X4 pairs of socks
- X4 pants
- Physio tape
- Coffee sachets

Sponsors

DHB supplied me with all my running kit for the JOGLE, which included the famous Visor! **www.wiggle.co.uk/dhb**

Precision Hydration provided me with electrolyte tablets (and lots of awesome freebies). They specialise in making personalised hydration plans for all types of athletes. **www.precisionhydration.com**

Resilient Nutrition make long range fuel which are basically delicious nut butter pouches that are brilliant for endurance events. **www.resilientnutrition.com**

Melio provide personalised health checks and with their support I was able to have a before and after blood test to show what endurance events can do to your body. *(see results on the next page)*. **www.meliohealth.co.uk**

Charity

The charity I chose to raise money for was the Forest Holme Hospice where Susan stayed during the end of her life. This hospice provided amazing support not only to Susan, but also her family.

If you would like to donate or find out more about Forest Holme Hospice, please go to **www.forestholmehospice.org.uk**

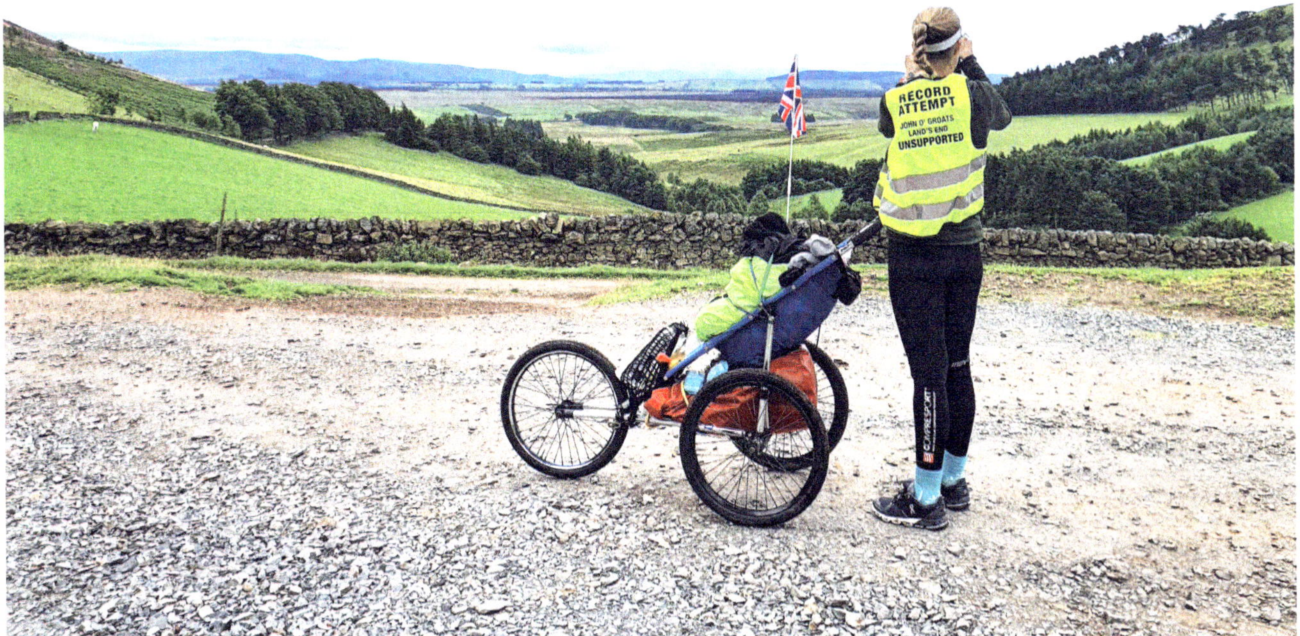
RECORD
ATTEMPT
JOHN O' GROATS
LAND'S END
UNSUPPORTED

Huge thanks to...

All the support, help and love from my best friend Claire. And to Selena, Paul, Tom and Olivier Northcott for everything they did.

Thanks to my awesome family for their constant support of my crazy challenges (I would promise that I won't do anymore, but we all know that would be a lie). Particularly my mum and Alan for everything they did for me during the challenge.

Gavin (and his lovely family) and Kathi for running my basecamp, for giving up so much of their time. And for their endless support before, during and after the challenge. You are both bloody brilliant people.

To MD for all the chats, laughs and good advice

My rock, Brutal Jim for the phone calls, visits and reminders that I had HUNDREDS OF MILES TO GO!

The Brutal Squirrel (Justin) for just being the Brutal Squirrel. You're the best!

Koen for his huge support and nightly check ins. And advice on my sore Achilles.

Ben for tracking the event (www.geotracks.co.uk) and giving me zero sympathy when I moaned about my feet. Also, thanks to his parents for coming to say hello and bringing me homemade biscuits

Martin 'have you done a Deca?' Curran and Steven for the huge support, Starbucks and Marmite Crisps

Matt and Karen for reminding me that I was an idiot and that this was all my own fault!

Pouch and family for the enormous cookies!

Darren Hardy for the use of his (amazing) RAB tent and sleeping mat.

Lee for opening his leisure centre at night so I could use a proper loo, have a cuppa and pitch my tent in the car park

Sarah Walsh and her partner for hours of great company and triathlon talk

Will Denny, who gave me Compeed and made me smile at the end of a long day

Gordon Graham for bringing me a Wigan Pie and for just being lovely

Martin Hill for not being a canal path murderer (and for the chocolate milkshake)

Matthew Pritchard and Lemmy for making me smile on a really shit day (and bringing me Twiglets)

Rob Seaman for his support (although I specifically said DON'T OPEN THE BAG!) and I'm sorry that you saw me at my most grumpiest!

Big Dave and Deca Dave for the Deca chats

Linn from Davis Chiropractics for all the pain and excellent treatment she continues to give me.

John Chambers for the use of his front garden after the Forth Bridge

Pete for the extra sleeping bag!

The crew of the Coast Guard near Perth That flyover made my day!

The photographer in the golf course who gave me crisps

The lovely family in Shrewsbury that cheered me up after my Sunday morning breakdown

Sub-3 Fiona, who distracted me for ages with tales of her super fast running

John, my 'petrol station angel' for helping me with the first puncture (and lending me his pump!)

JOGLE Mick for all his pre-event advice

My Land's End rent-a-crowd lead by the lovely Debbie Butt

The man at the petrol station who gave me his reward cards from Greggs so I could get 2 free coffees as 'I deserved them more than he did'

The guy who picked me up from the station in Scotland and took me to the start

The family who gave me some cheese and crisps in Scotland

The lovely woman in the shop who wouldn't let me pay for my food

The Running Granny for the chat and scones.

Thanks to Thomas Sneddon and Steven Howell for giving me support when I was on the verge (of the A9)

To Chris Lakey and his partner (sorry I was moaning about the traffic!)

The lovely Ginny for being such wonderful company and support

Thank you Carol for the awesome photos

To the Brutal Duathlon man who had AMAZING coffee and posh chocolate biscuits

The ladies from the pub who gave me boiled eggs and cheddars! And the offer of a hot shower too…

Susan Grey for giving up her afternoon and setting up a little picnic for me. And for making me feel better,

Wendy, for running miles to come and say hello!

Matthew (Beard!) for meeting me and chatting about all things Enduroman

A HUGE thanks to the guy who fixed my broken axle (Man of Ross). You'll probably never fully understand how much I appreciated your help that morning.

Paul from Forest Holme Hospice for all his support and the post-JOGLE Latte

Thanks to all the farmers whose fields I slept in, whether they knew it or not. And especially the farmer who didn't murder me with a crowbar. And the infant school that lent me their bike shed for the night (unbeknownst to them).

Thanks to the staff of Premier Inn that let me dry my clothes and buggy when everything was absolutely soaked.

To Jordan Wylie, who was also at Land's End on his epic Paddle Board around the UK, for stopping and congratulating me on my finish (www.thegreatbritishpaddle.com) and also Speedo Mick for coming to say well done.

Thanks to the man in the kiosk at Land's End who let me jump the (very long) queue.

To the amazing Pip Hare for her generosity and support

To Talan for being a constant inspiration

DS, there aren't many people like you in the world. Thank you for everything.

And to the guy who quietly supported me from a distance.

A massive thanks to all the people who clapped, cheered, messaged me, supported via social media, gave me food and cups of tea, made me laugh and helped out in any way they could.

And finally, thank you to Susan Northcott. Although I'm not in the least bit religious, I always felt her around me during the JOGLE. Her love and support were a constant presence.

Apologies if I've missed anyone (I have a terrible memory), but I am sincerely grateful to every single person who took time out of their day to support me and make this challenge possible.

Additional photography by Gavin Jeffers, Kathi Harman and Carol Cotterill

Claire Smith is an ultra-endurance athlete and event organiser. She set up Brutal Events in 2011, widely regarded as the world's hardest extreme triathlons (www.brutalevents.co.uk).

Claire has completed many ultra-distance events and is the first British woman to finish a Double Deca Triathlon. She is the current self-supported JOGLE World Record holder.

When she is not organising events, Claire works as a graphic and website designer. She lives in Bournemouth with her two children.

BRUTAL CLAIRE
ULTRA ENDURANCE ATHLETE

www.brutalclaire.co.uk

Printed in Great Britain
by Amazon